A human righ

on reducing restrictive practices
in intellectual disability
and autism

Edited by Sam Karim

British Library Cataloguing in Publication Data

A CIP record for this book is available from the Public Library

© BILD Publications 2014

BILD Publications is the imprint of:
British Institute of Learning Disabilities
Birmingham Research Park
97 Vincent Drive
Edgbaston
Birmingham B15 2SQ

Telephone: 0121 415 6960
E-mail: enquiries@bild.org.uk
Website: www.bild.org.uk

ISBN 978 1 905218 34 9

BILD Publications are distributed by:
BookSource
50 Cambuslang Road
Cambuslang
Glasgow G32 8NB

Telephone: 0845 370 0067
Fax: 0845 370 0068

For a publications catalogue with details of all BILD books and journals e-mail enquiries@bild.org.uk or visit the BILD website www.bild.org.uk

Printed in the UK by Latimer Trend and Company Ltd, Plymouth

People with learning disabilities and people with autism want to make their own choices and decisions about the things that affect their lives. To help make this happen, BILD works to influence policy-makers and campaigns for change, and our services can help organisations improve their service design and develop their staff to deliver great support.

Contents

Editor

Sam Karim   Barrister, Kings Chambers, Manchester, UK

Contributors

Bob Bowen   Adjunct Assistant Professor of Psychiatry at the University of
               Rochester Medical Centre, School of Medicine and Dentistry,
               Rochester, NY, USA

Mathieu   Public Law Solicitor, Irwin Mitchell Solicitors, Manchester, UK
Culverhouse

Jeffery Chan   Chief Practitioner, Yooralla, Victoria, Adjunct Professor,
               University of Queensland, Australia

Phillip French Director, Australian Centre for Disability Law, Sydney, Australia

Simon Kemp   Senior Vice President of North America Development,
               The Mandt System Inc, Texas, USA

Lynne Webber   Practice Leader, Research and Service Development, Office
               of Professional Practice, Department of Human Services,
               Melbourne, Australia, Clinical Associate Professor, School
               of Psychology, Deakin University, Victoria, Australia

Sharon Paley   Director of Clinical Innovation and Governance, Centre of
               Excellence for Clinical Innovation and Behaviour Support,
               Department of Communities, Child Safety and Disability
               Services, Brisbane, Australia

Introduction

Sam Karim

I have worked with individuals with a learning disability and/or autism for over a decade in a legal context, the main concerns that are regularly raised by people is the thin, yet significant line that divides the ethical and legal use of restraint and seclusion and abusive and illegal practices. There are also additional concerns that are raised by people relating to a deprivation of liberty in line with Article 5 of the *European Convention on Human Rights* (Council of Europe, 2002) ('the ECHR').

The case of *A Local Authority v C* [2011] EWHC 1539 (Admin) ('the C case') exemplified these concerns. This case was a stark reminder of the practical difficulties that health, social care and education providers face in understanding and managing challenging behaviour within a legal context. The decision of the Court of Protection and the Administrative Court by Mr Justice Ryder (now Lord Justice Ryder) clarified how family members and advocates of young people, or adults with learning disabilities or autism, should expect them to be treated.

For the purpose of background and context to the C case, in England and Wales a deprivation of liberty under Article 5 of the ECHR is unlawful unless it is authorised by the Court of Protection, or via a paper based exercise known as the Standard Authorisation, that adheres to the Mental Capacity Act 2005 ('the 2005 Act'). Guidance in relation to support for people with mental health needs issued by the Department of Health (2008) defines seclusion in the *Code of Practice: Mental Health Act 1983*, as:

> … the supervised confinement of a patient in a room. Its sole aim
> is to contain severely disturbed behaviour which is likely to cause
> harm to others. (Page 34)

The *Code of Practice: Mental Health Act 1983* also states that prolonged or repeated use of seclusion would be an indication to consider formal detention and states the importance of distinguishing between seclusion and the use of time out, and other behavioural and psychological therapies.

These issues came to the forefront in the case of C who was severely autistic and had profound learning disabilities. His behaviour also challenged the service that supported him. C's behaviour was suggested to be uncontrollable and as a result, this was largely managed by the use of a padded blue room in which he was secluded when exhibiting challenging behaviours such as defecating, smearing and drinking and eating his own urine and faeces, aggression and stripping naked. He was not permitted to leave the blue room when this happened. The court was required to consider a number of issues; most significantly what was the good practice to be adopted in relation to his nakedness and the use of seclusion and restraint, particularly the impact that the blue room had on his quality of life and wellbeing. In considering this the court had to decide whether C was subjected to inhuman and degrading treatment and also whether his right to liberty and respect for his private life had been infringed. The court also noted that if the blue room was to be used, the school had to be clear it was only for as long as was necessary, it was proportionate and that it was the least restrictive option. The judge confirmed that an *"intervention and prevention plan for the use of the blue room and a document advising upon the management of C's nakedness is to be agreed."* He also confirmed that seclusion was not to be used solely for the reason of his nakedness, or as a punishment to manage C's behaviour or on the basis that C was self harming. Mr Justice Ryder concluded:

> *"As a consequence of the findings, decisions and approvals made by the court, detailed orders and declarations under the Mental Capacity Act 2005 have been made providing for C's interim placement at the school but under very clearly defined procedures and constraints, in particular, concerning his seclusion. His liberty may be deprived in very limited circumstances and only with the authority of this court."*

This case is a good starting point for a book that is considering the legal and ethical use of restraint and seclusion. It highlighted the seriousness of the overarching principle that a person who lacks capacity should not be deprived of their liberty, apart from in the most exceptional circumstances where it is considered to be in that person's best interests.

Such a statement is not without authority. In the *Report of the Special Rapporteur on Torture and other Cruel, Inhuman or Degrading Treatment or Punishment, Juan E Mendez*, the United Nations (2013) concluded that where relevant:

"... both prolonged seclusion and restraint may constitute torture and ill-treatment… The Special Rapporteur has addressed the issue of solitary confinement and stated that its imposition, of any duration, on persons with mental disabilities is cruel, inhuman or degrading treatment." (Page 14)

This report called for Member States to impose an absolute ban on the use of restraint and solitary confinement, for both long and short term application. Indeed, it is now well established that restraint on people with disabilities for even a short period of time may constitute torture and ill-treatment, see *Bures v Czech Republic*, Application No. 37679/08 ECHR (2012).

In practice, it is interesting to note that Romijn and Freveriks (2012) found that in the United Kingdom restraints are still commonly used in the care of people with an intellectual disability.

Against this backdrop, this book for a national and international audience aims to promote good practice in reducing the use of restrictive practices in the support of children and adults with intellectual disabilities, including learning disabilities and autism. The book considers in detail the legal and ethical principles underpinning good practice and is suitable for legal, education, health and social care professionals, and all those involved in supporting people with disabilities. This book explores international approaches, in order to set out good practice principles.

The first chapter in this book by Sam Karim and Mathieu Culverhouse, *Legal reflections on the human rights of restraint reduction*, focuses on the legislative framework in England and Wales and describes in detail the statutory provisions and guidance relating to reducing the use of restrictive practices. The chapter specifically describes cases relating to human rights legislation.

The second chapter by Jeffrey Chan, Lynne Webber and Phillip French, *The importance of safeguarding rights and the role of legislation: the Australian perspective*, introduces the reader to a different legislative framework in the state of Victoria, Australia. This innovative framework specifically protects the human rights of people with disabilities who are subject to restrictive practices. It also puts in place strategic initiatives to monitor and reduce the use of restrictive practices.

The third chapter by Sharon Paley, *Ethical principles and good practice in reducing restrictive practices*, explores the ethical issues to consider when seeking to reduce the use of restrictive practice. Paley introduces a positive behaviour support model for ethical decision making.

The fourth chapter by Bob Bowen and Simon Kemp, *Replacing restraint: good practices in North American human service programmes for persons with intellectual disabilities and autism*, takes a broader perspective and describes examples of good practice in North America on reducing the use of restrictive practice.

The fifth chapter by Lynne Webber, Jeffrey Chan and Phillip French, *Good practices in Australia in the use of restraint reduction practices for people with intellectual disabilities and autism*, describes in detail some of the specific initiatives brought in by the Disability Act 2006, in the state of Victoria, Australia, to protect the rights of people with disabilities who are subject to restrictive interventions. In particular, the chapter explores the role of the Senior Practitioner, the need to report any use of restrictive physical interventions, the use of behaviour support plans and training for staff in services.

Finally, I wish to thank the contributors to the book, each highly experienced in the topic that they have covered. Without their international perspectives, I would have not been able to outline what I consider to be good practice. I remain indebted to each contributor. We have endeavoured to state, where applicable, the law and policy as at 1 April 2014.

Sam Karim

References

A Local Authority v C [2011] EWHC 1539 (Admin)

Bures v Czech Republic, Application No. 37679/08 ECHR (2012)

Council of Europe (2002) *European Convention on Human Rights Protocol 13.* Strasbourg: Council of Europe

Department for Constitutional Affairs (2005) *Mental Capacity Act 2005.* Download from www.legislation.gov.uk

Department of Health (2008) *Code of Practice: Mental Health Act 1983.* London: TSO

Romijn, A and Freveriks, J M (2012) Restriction on restraints in the care for people with intellectual disabilities in the Netherlands: lessons learned from Australia, UK, and United States. *Journal of Policy and Practice in Intellectual Disabilities,* 9(2),127–133

United Nations General Assembly (2013) *Report of the Special Rapporteur on Torture and other Cruel, Inhuman or Degrading Treatment or Punishment, Juan E Mendez.* New York: United Nations

Chapter 1:

Legal reflections on the human rights of restraint reduction

Sam Karim and Mathieu Culverhouse

Part 1: Ethics, statutory provisions and guidance

"The key principles underpinning the guidance:

- Compliance with the relevant rights in the European Convention on Human Rights at all times

- Understanding people's behaviour allows their unique needs, aspirations, experiences and strengths to be recognised and their quality of life to be enhanced

- Involvement and participation of people with care and support needs, their families, carers and advocates is essential, wherever practicable and subject to the person's wishes and confidentiality obligations

- People must be treated with compassion, dignity and kindness

- Health and social care services must support people to balance safety from harm and freedom of choice

- Positive relationships between the people who deliver services and the people they support must be protected and preserved."

Department of Health (2014) Page 16

The purpose of this chapter is to consider the legal parameters of restraint and seclusion in England and Wales. Part 1 considers the relevant statutory provisions and guidance. Part 2 gives an overview of human rights laws and considers relevant case law to demonstrate what amounts to 'lawful' restraint or seclusion, and when such practices amount to a deprivation of liberty.

Before one undertakes such a task, a brief overview of the ethical underpinnings is necessary.

Restraint reduction: ethical justification

A proper starting point for considering restraint reduction must be Paley's chapter (Paley, 2009) on seclusion and time out. She sets out three possible rationales for the use of seclusion:

- **Positive therapy** – to help a person to calm more quickly and enable them to learn to 'manage' their own emotional states by reflecting on their behaviour and emotional expression. This approach sees seclusion as leading to some kind of beneficial therapeutic change in the individual.

- **Containment** – placing a person in a room alone preventing them from harming others in a time of crisis. As above, this approach sees seclusion as leading to some kind of beneficial therapeutic change in the individual.

- **Punishment** – seclusion is seen as an intentional aversive intervention, the intention being to withdraw the individual from all positive experiences.

Literature has confirmed, see for instance Lyon and Pimor (2004), that seclusion should only be used in extreme cases; and as such, it is an emergency procedure to be implemented only when there is significant risk. Nelstrop et al (2006) conclude that there was insufficient evidence to support seclusion (or restraint) being safe or effective in the short-term management of people in psychiatric settings. It is clear that a restrictive physical intervention carries increased risk; the use of seclusion or 'time out' may also increase the risk to an individual.

The legal parameters: the law in England and Wales

When looking at the use of restraint practices in relation to people who lack capacity, it is vital to consider the legal framework and background in which any form of restraint is used.

The Court of Protection

The jurisdiction of the Court of Protection is defined by the provisions of the Mental Capacity Act 2005 which came into force in 2007 in England and Wales. A decision made by the court under the Mental Capacity Act (MCA 2005) must be in the best interests of the protected person, P. Section 1(6) of the MCA 2005 says that, "*before the act is done or the decision is made, regard must be had to whether the purpose for which it is needed can be as effectively achieved in a way that is less restrictive of the person's rights and freedom of action.*" The Act is generally only concerned with persons over the age of 16, although provision is made (in Section 21 and regulations therein) for the transfer of proceedings relating to 16 and 17 year olds. For children below the age of 16 years of age a similar scheme is followed under the Children Act 1989. For instance, a statutory order can be sought under the Children Act 1989 (Section 25) for an authorisation to keep a child in secure accommodation.

There is power in section 48 of the MCA 2005 to grant interim declarations provided that the relevant person lacks capacity in relation to the matter and it is in the best interests of that person to make the order or make the directions without delay.

The manner in which a best interest decision is to be made by a decision maker, including the court, is addressed in Section 4. Section 4(2) states that a court must consider all the relevant circumstances and Section 4(4) says so far as is reasonably practicable; the court must permit and encourage the person concerned to participate in the decision affecting him. Section 4(6) which deals with *P*'s past and present wishes and feelings, beliefs and values and other factors which *P* would be likely to consider if he were able to do so.

The court is not obliged to give effect to the decision which *P* would have arrived at if he had capacity to make the decision for himself and was acting reasonably (sometimes referred to as a 'substituted judgement'), but rather it applies an objective test as to what is in his best interests taking into consideration the factors which *P* would be likely to have considered if he had capacity including what *P* would have decided if that can be deduced. Section 4(7) states that the court must take into account, if it is practicable and appropriate to consult them, the views of other persons.

Lack of capacity

A person is considered to lack capacity according to section 2 of the Act where:

> "at the material time he is unable to make a decision for himself in relation to the matter because of an impairment of, or a disturbance in the functioning of, the mind or brain."

Section 2 applies when a person cannot understand the information relevant to the decision, retain that information, use or weigh that information or communicate his decision. The Act sets out various additional rules about how these matters are determined (Section 3), as well as various rules about what must and must not be taken into account when determining 'best interests' (Section 4).

Examples of an impairment or disturbance in the functioning of the mind or brain may include: some forms of mental illness; dementia; significant learning disabilities and the symptoms of alcohol or drug abuse. A person's capacity concerns his ability to make a specific decision. It would be contrary to the guiding principles of the MCA 2005 to make blanket findings as to a person's capacity. For example, in the community care context, rather than ask simply whether a person 'lacks capacity', it will be necessary to ask whether the person has capacity to determine where he should live, what sort of care he wishes to receive and when, if moving to residential care, he wished to be visited by his family. Questions about capacity, therefore, need to be 'person' and 'decision' specific.

Best interests

All acts and decisions made on behalf of a person who lacks capacity should be taken in his or her best interests. This requirement encompasses a wide range of medical, emotional and welfare issues.

Section 4 of the MCA 2005 sets out a checklist of factors that must always be considered in determining the best interests of a person lacking capacity. The decision maker must, among other things:

- consider whether it is likely that a person will at some time have capacity in relation to the matter in question and, if so, when that is likely to be; it may be that the decision should be deferred, to enable the person to gain or regain capacity

- so far as reasonably practicable, permit and encourage the person to participate, or improve his ability to participate, as fully as possible in the decision, even though he is unable to make the decision himself

- consider the person's past and present wishes and feelings, in particular any relevant written statement made while the person had capacity

- consider the person's beliefs, values and other factors that would have been likely to influence his decision if he had capacity, eg cultural background, religious and political beliefs

- consult with appropriate persons, eg anyone engaged in caring for the person, anyone with a lasting power of attorney and any deputy appointed for the person by the Court of Protection

The role of the Court of Protection

The Court of Protection has now taken over the functions of the High Court's inherent jurisdiction to determine questions concerning the capacity of adults and the best interests of adults lacking capacity. That jurisdiction was described by Munby J as follows:

> "It is now clear ...that the court exercises what is, in substance and reality, a jurisdiction in relation to incompetent adults which is for all practical purposes indistinguishable from its well established parens patriae or wardship jurisdictions in relation to children. The court exercises a 'protective jurisdiction' in relation to vulnerable adults just as it does in relation to wards of court."

> A Local Authority v MA, NA and SA (by her children's guardian LJ) [2005] EWHC 2942 (Fam)

The court can regulate everything that contributes to the incompetent adult's welfare and happiness.

The core jurisdiction of the court is conferred by Section 16 of the MCA 2005, which empowers it to make substituted decisions for persons lacking capacity, applying the principles of the Act. Section 17 provides a number of particular instances:

- deciding where the person is to live

- what contact he is to have with specified persons

- making an order prohibiting a named person from having contact with the person

- giving or refusing consent to medical treatment

Notable recent disputes have concerned the removal of individuals from the family home to residential care homes and whether this constitutes a mere restriction, which is now authorised under Section 6 of the Act, or engages Article 5 of the European Convention on Human Rights ('ECHR') as an unlawful deprivation of liberty. In *JE v Surrey County Council* [2006] EWHC 3459 (Fam) there was a finding of deprivation of liberty where a vulnerable adult was admitted to a residential care home, contrary to his wife's wishes and without a declaration of the court. More cases relating to the above can be found further in this chapter.

The Government has proposed remedying the problem identified in *JE v Surrey County Council* [2006] through amendments to the Act, based on an admissions procedure for care homes to be supervised by the local authority and independent mental capacity advocates.

Part 2: Human rights and case law of England and Wales

Human rights jurisprudence

Having considered the ethical, statutory and policy underpinning of the use of restraint and seclusion, it is imperative that one has some understanding of the human rights agenda, before one considers the concept of a 'deprivation of liberty'. In England and Wales this principally takes form in the Human Rights Act 1998 (HRA 1998) incorporating the European Convention on Human Rights (ECHR). The same principles apply to all member states of the European Union, who are a party to the ECHR.

The HRA 1998 was enacted over a decade ago. It is now a well-established part of the English and Welsh legal backdrop. The key provisions include:

- Section 2 requires that a court or tribunal determining a question under the HRA 1998, in connection with a Convention right, to take account of any jurisprudence or decision of the Strasbourg institutions.

- Section 3 sets out the interpretative obligation requiring the courts to read, and give effect to, legislation in a way which is compatible with those Convention rights, so far as it is possible to do so.

- Section 4 outlines the ability to seek and obtain a declaration of incompatibility if legislation cannot be interpreted compatibly with Convention.

- Section 6 makes it unlawful for a public authority to act in a way which is incompatible with a Convention right unless it could not have acted differently as a result of a statutory provision.

The 'rights and fundamental freedoms' which are protected by the ECHR as enshrined by the HRA 1998 include:

Article 2:	**the right to life**
Article 3:	**prohibition of torture**
Article 5:	**the right to liberty and security**
Article 6:	**the right to a fair trial**
Article 8:	**the right to respect for private and family life, the home and correspondence**
Article 9:	**the right to freedom of thought, conscience and religion**
Article 10:	**freedom of expression**
Article 11:	**freedom of assembly and association**
Article 12:	**the right to marry**
Article 14:	**the prohibition of discrimination in respect of Article rights**
Article 1, 1st Protocol:	**the protection of property**

The courts of England and Wales, when considering a claim that a public authority has acted unlawfully by breaching a Convention right, are required to take into account the Strasbourg jurisprudence. At present where there is established Strasbourg jurisprudence on an Article right, the court will effectively be required to adopt that interpretation. The Supreme Court (previously the House of Lords) in a succession of cases has explained the nature of the obligations relating to Section 2 of the HRA 1998:

R (Ullah) v Special Adjudicator [2004] UKHL 26, Lord Bingham of Cornhill stated at [20] that:

"It is of course open to member states to provide for rights more generous than those guaranteed by the Convention, but such provision should not be the product of interpretation of the Convention by national courts, since the meaning of the Convention should be uniform throughout the states party to it. The duty of national courts is to keep pace with the Strasbourg jurisprudence as it evolves over time: no more, but certainly no less."

R v Chief Constable of South Yorkshire Police ex p LS and Marper [2004] UKHL 39, Lord Steyn stated at [27]:

"While I would not wish to subscribe to all the generalisations in the Court of Appeal about cultural traditions in the United Kingdom, in comparison with other European states, I do accept that when one moves on to consider the question of objective justification under Article 8(2) the cultural traditions in the United Kingdom are material. With great respect to Lord Woolf the same is not true under Article 8(1). [Lord Steyn then set out Lord Bingham's speech above in Ullah] ... The question whether the retention of fingerprints and samples engages Article 8(1) should receive a uniform interpretation throughout member states, unaffected by different cultural traditions. And the current Strasbourg view, as reflected in decisions of the Commission, ought to be taken into account."

Box 3

R (Animal Defenders International) v Secretary of State for Culture, Media and Sport [2008] UKHL 15. Lord Scott expressed his opinion that it would be possible for the domestic courts to have a divergence of view from the European Court of Human Rights (the ECtHR) on the meaning of Article rights. He stated at Paragraph 44:

"The result of the present appeal to this House shows, therefore, no more than the possibility of a divergence between the opinion of the European Court as to the application of Article 10 in relation to the statutory prohibition of which Animal Defence International complains and the opinion of this House. The possibility of such a divergence is contemplated, implicitly at least, by the 1998 Act. The 1998 Act incorporated into domestic law the articles of the Convention and of the Protocols set out in Schedule 1 to the Act. So the articles became part of domestic law. But the incorporated articles are not merely part of domestic law. They remain, as they were before the 1998 Act, articles of a Convention binding on the United Kingdom under international law. In so far as the articles are part of domestic law, this House is, and, when this House is eventually replaced by a Supreme Court, that court will be, the court of final appeal whose interpretation of the incorporated articles will, subject only to legislative intervention, be binding in domestic law. In so far as the articles are part of international law they are binding on the United Kingdom as a signatory of the Convention and the European Court is, for the purposes of international law, the final arbiter of their meaning and effect. Section 2 of the 1998 Act requires any domestic court determining a question which has arisen in connection with a Convention right to take into account, inter alia, 'any judgment, decision, declaration or advisory opinion of the European Court of Human Rights' (Section (1)(a)). The judgments of the European Court are, therefore, not binding on domestic courts. They constitute material, very important material, that must be taken into account, but domestic courts are nonetheless not bound by the European Court's interpretation of an incorporated article."

Box 4

R (Pretty) v Director of Public Prosecutions (Secretary of State for the Home Department Intervening) [2002] 1 AC 800, where the House of Lords held Article 8 was directed to the protection of personal autonomy while the person was alive but did not confer a right to decide when or how to die. The European Court of Human Rights in *Pretty v United Kingdom* (2002) 35 EHRR 1 disagreed. At Paragraphs 65 and 67 the Court said that:

"The very essence of the Convention is respect for human dignity and human freedom. Without in any way negating the principle of sanctity of life protected under the Convention, the court considers that it is under Article 8 that notions of the quality of life take on significance. In an era of growing medical sophistication combined with longer life expectancies, many people are concerned that they should not be forced to linger on in old age or in states of advanced physical or mental decrepitude which conflict with strongly held ideas of self and personal identity… The applicant in this case is prevented by law from exercising her choice to avoid what she considers will be an undignified and distressing end to her life. The court is not prepared to exclude that this constitutes an interference with her right to respect for private life as guaranteed under Article 8(1) of the Convention. It considers below whether this interference conforms with the requirements of the second Paragraph of Article 8."

Box 5

R (on the application of Purdy) (Appellant) v Director of Public Prosecutions (Respondent) [2009] EWCA Civ 92, the Court of Appeal held that it was bound to follow the decision of the House of Lords and was not at liberty to apply the ruling of the Strasbourg court; and

In the House of Lords in *R (on the application of Purdy) (Appellant) v Director of Public Prosecutions (Respondent)* [2009] UKHL 45, Lord Hope said at Paragraph 34 that:

"The House is, of course, free to depart from its earlier decision and to follow that of the Strasbourg court. As Lord Bingham said in R (Ullah) v Special Adjudicator [2004] UKHL 26, [2004] 2 AC 323, Paragraph 20, it is ordinarily the clear duty of our domestic courts to give practical recognition to the principles laid down by the Strasbourg court as governing the Convention rights as the effectiveness of the Convention as an international instrument depends on the loyal acceptance by member states of the principles that, as the highest authority on the interpretation of those rights, it lays down… But it is obvious that the interests of human rights law would not be well served if the House were to regard itself as bound by a previous decision as to the meaning or effect of a Convention right which was shown to be inconsistent with a subsequent decision in Strasbourg. Otherwise the House would be at risk of endorsing decisions which are incompatible with Convention rights.

The duty under Section 6 makes it unlawful to act incompatibly with Convention rights only, applies to a 'public authority'. Section 6(3) of the HRA 1998 provides that a 'public authority' includes not only a court or tribunal under Section 6(3)(a), but also, '(b) any person certain of whose functions are functions of a public nature.' What is a public authority has been the subject of litigation and the interface of public authorities and private providers remains a live topic."

Box 6

In *YL v Birmingham City Council* [2007] UKHL 27 the majority of the House of Lords concluded that an independent provider of health and social care services housing an 84-year-old woman with Alzheimer's disease in a nursing home was not a public authority for the purposes of the HRA 1998. The court was particularly influenced by the fact that Southern Cross, the nursing home provider was a private, profit-earning company, acting for private and commercial gain, and merely contracting with a local authority to provide a service. The majority view in this case was consistent with the earlier decision in *Cameron v Network Rail (Infrastructure Ltd)* [2007] 1 WLR 163. The court reinforced that it was necessary to examine the context in which a contractor was acting, and the basis upon which the contractor was acting, and the key focus had to be on the nature of the functions it was undertaking. In contrast, both Lord Bingham and Baroness Hale concluded that the type of situation Southern Cross was in was precisely that designed to be covered by Section 6(3)(b), where a private body was performing an important public function of the provision of care, albeit pursuant to contractual arrangements.

This case has clear consequences. Individuals placed in privately run-care homes by a local authority as required by the National Assistance Act 1948 cannot directly invoke the provisions of the Convention against the care home provider itself. Such providers are not public authorities for the purposes of the HRA 1998. Individuals do, however, have an arguable course of action against a local authority if they fail to enforce the terms of the contract between themselves and private care homes. Those terms should include that they ought to abide by the HRA 1998.

Box 7

The case of *London and Quadrant Housing Trust v R on the application of Weaver and the Equality and Human Rights Commission* [2009] EWCA Civ 597 applied the judgement from the case *YL v Birmingham City Council* [2007] UKHL 27 and found that the termination of a tenancy and the seeking of possession on the grounds of non payment of rent in respect of social housing could not properly be categorised as an exercise of a public nature. Rather it was a private act arising out of a contract. Whether the landlord as a registered social landlord was a public authority so that when terminating the tenancy of someone in social housing that act was subject to human rights principles and a public law challenge was rejected in the circumstances of the case. Again, the importance of context was emphasised.

The Convention rights

What follows is a brief outline of the Convention rights which are frequently used in judicial review claims, in the Court of Protection and more generally:

Box 1

Article 2: *in R(L) (A Patient) v Secretary of State for the Home Department* [2007] EWCA Civ 767, the Court of Appeal confirmed that the rights under Article 2 extended not only to accountability of the state for the death of a person or serious injury while in state custody, but also to an investigation of the facts and explanation of how the death or serious injury occurred. The mere fact of such a death or serious injury obliged the state to commence an independent investigation, and in cases of serious injury, the necessity for a further public hearing would depend on whether it appeared to the independent investigator that the state or its agents potentially bore responsibility for the injury. An internal prison investigation of the attempted suicide of a young person held on remand in Feltham was insufficient to comply with Article 2.

Recently in *R (Smith) v Oxfordshire Assistant Deputy Coroner* [2009] EWCA Civ 441, the Court of Appeal held that the State was bound to conduct an investigation into the death of a conscript to satisfy Article 2.

Box 2

Article 3 is well known. Recently in *R (AM) v SOSHD* [2009] EWCA Civ 219, the Court of Appeal indicated that the possibility of inmates at the privately run immigration detention centre having suffered inhuman and degrading treatment triggered the State's duties of investigation under Article 3 and that such duties were not affected by the possibility of a criminal investigation or the bringing of civil proceedings.

Box 3

Article 5 is no better exemplified than the recent control order litigation. In *Secretary of State for the Home Department SSHD v JJ* [2007] UKHL 45, control orders were imposed on individuals resulting in an effective curfew upon them for 18 hours a day and exclusion of visitors. The House of Lords dismissed the SSHD's appeal against the quashing of those orders and concluded that the overall effect of the orders did amount to a deprivation of liberty for the purposes of Article 5. Lord Brown made clear his view that a curfew of 16 hours a day was the maximum permitted before Article 5 was infringed. See also *Secretary of State for the Home Department v E* [2007] UKHL 47, where a 12 hour curfew was held to be insufficiently stringent to infringe Article 5.

More recently, in *R (James) v Secretary of State for Justice* [2009] UKHL 22, the House of Lords held that Article 5(4) was only engaged in public protection sentences so as to ensure that a court (the Parole Board) should speedily decide whether a prisoner continued to be lawfully detained: that would continue to be the case unless and until it was satisfied of his safety for release or that so long had elapsed without any effective review of his dangerousness that there was a breach of Article 5(1).

Box 4

Article 6: in *R (Wright) v Secretary of State for Health* [2007] EWCA Civ 999, the Court of Appeal held that the denial of a right to make representations before a care worker, which is provisionally included on a list of persons considered unsuitable to work with children, held by the Secretary of State under section 82 of the Care Standards Act 2000, was in breach of a care worker's rights under Article 6. Moreover, that breach was not cured by the fact that the care worker had an opportunity to seek to persuade the Secretary of State to remove him/her from the list, to seek judicial review of the decision to include the worker on the list, or to appeal under Section 86 of the CSA. May LJ stated at Paragraph 37 that,

"...Article 6 is infringed because the worker does not get any hearing, let alone a fair and public one within a reasonable time. Possibilities of judicial review are not sufficient to achieve compliance with Article 6..."

Box 5

Article 8: the right to respect for private and family life, home and correspondence has a broad application. In *Société Colas Est v France* (2004) 39 EHRR 17 the court accepted that raids carried out by official inspectors on company premises were capable of engaging the company's rights to a 'home' within the meaning, Article 8(1). This was reinforced in *Buck v Germany* [2005] ECHR 41604/98 at [31] and *Kent Pharmaceuticals Ltd v UK* no 9355/03, 11 October 2005. See also *Wieser and Bicos Beteiligungen GMBH v Austria* [2007] ECHR 74336/01 (16 October 2007), when the court found violations of Article 8 in respect of the search and seizure of data belonging both to a lawyer and a company.

In R(Countryside Alliance) per Lord Bingham said:

"The content of this right has been described as 'elusive' and does not lend itself to exhaustive definition. This may help to explain why the right is expressed as one to respect, as contrasted with the more categorical language used in other articles. But the purpose of the article is in my view clear. It is to protect the individual against intrusion by agents of the state, unless for good reason, into the private sphere within which individuals expect to be left alone to conduct their personal affairs and live their personal lives as they choose."

English courts have been more reluctant than the European Court of Human Rights to interpret Strasbourg jurisprudence as extending the scope of Article 8. See *R v Attorney General and Anor ex p. Countryside Alliance* [2007] UKHL 52 where the House of Lords refused to find a breach of Article 8. The claimant argued infringement of private life and autonomy in reliance on *Pretty v UK* (2002) 35 EHRR 1 and the ECtHR's finding. See also the House of Lords 2009 decision in *Purdy*.

Note the recent case of *R (G) v Nottinghamshire Healthcare NHS Trust* [2009] EWCA Civ 795 (CA) where the Court of Appeal concluded that a smoking ban at a special hospital did not have a sufficiently adverse effect on a patient's physical or mental integrity as to engage Article 8. Even if Article 8 had been engaged, the court indicated that the ban was justified under Article 8(2).

Box 7

Article 10: in *R (Animal Defenders International) v Secretary of State for Culture, Media and Sport* [2008] UKHL 15, Lord Bingham stated:

"The weight to be accorded to the judgment of Parliament depends on the circumstances and the subject matter. In the present context it should in my opinion be given great weight, for three main reasons. First, it is reasonable to expect that our democratically-elected politicians will be peculiarly sensitive to the measures necessary to safeguard the integrity of our democracy. It cannot be supposed that others, including judges, will be more so. Secondly, Parliament has resolved, uniquely since the 1998 Act came into force in October 2000, that the prohibition of political advertising on television and radio may possibly, although improbably, infringe Article 10 but has nonetheless resolved to proceed under Section 19(1)(b) of the Act. It has done so, while properly recognising the interpretative supremacy of the European Court, because of the importance which it attaches to maintenance of this prohibition. The judgment of Parliament on such an issue should not be lightly overridden. Thirdly, legislation cannot be framed so as to address particular cases. It must lay down general rules ....A general rule means that a line must be drawn, and it is for Parliament to decide where. The drawing of a line inevitably means that hard cases will arise falling on the wrong side of it, but that should not be held to invalidate the rule if, judged in the round, it is beneficial."

Box 8

Article 12: in *R (Baiai) v Secretary of State for the Home Department (Nos 1 and 2)* [2007] EWCA Civ 478, the Court of Appeal considered a regime requiring a person subject to immigration control who wished to enter into a civil marriage in the UK to seek a certificate of approval from the Secretary of State. The court found the particular regime created to be incompatible with the right to marry under Article 12.

Box 9

Article 14 provides that:

"The enjoyment of the rights and freedoms set forth in this Convention shall be secured without discrimination on any ground such as sex, race, colour, language, political or other opinion, national or social origin, association with a national minority, property, birth or other status."

This is not a free-standing provision. It prohibits discrimination only in the enjoyment of the rights and freedoms in the Convention. Equally, it is does not require any other Article to be violated.

In relation to the term 'other status' note *Kjeldsen, Busk Madsen and Pedersen v Denmark* (1976) 1 EHRR 711, Paragraph 56, the ECtHR referred to *"discriminatory treatment having as its basis or reason a personal characteristic ('status') by which persons or groups of persons are distinguishable from each other."*

In *R(S) v Chief Constable of the South Yorkshire Police* [2004] UKHL 39, the House of Lords adopted the requirement to identify a 'personal characteristic', and not to treat the list as open-ended.

The 'personal characteristic' requirement has also been applied by the Court of Appeal in *R(RJM) v Secretary of State for Work and Pensions* [2007] EWCA Civ 614. The court also concluded that 'other status' in Article 14 depended upon a personal characteristic, but rejected the notion that the nature of the personal characteristic must necessarily be involuntary.

Box 10

Article 1, 1st Protocol: in *R(Malik) v Waltham Forest NHS Primary Care Trust* [2007] 1 WLR 2092, the Court of Appeal found that inclusion of a doctor's name on a list of those qualified to work locally for the NHS was effectively a licence to render services to the public. As it was not transferable or marketable, it was found not to be a possession for the purposes of Article 1, 1st Protocol. The mere prospect of future loss could not amount to a possession for that purpose where such clientele/goodwill did not exist. An individual's monetary loss of future livelihood could not, on its own, constitute a possession.

So what amounts to a deprivation of liberty in respect of Article 5 of the Convention?

The fifth guiding principle of the Mental Capacity Act 2005 is that before a decision is made or an act is done, regard must be had to whether the purpose for which it is needed can be as effectively achieved in a way that is less restrictive of the person's rights and freedom of action. In short, any limitations placed on a person's rights must be both necessary and proportionate. For the purposes of Section 5, Mental Capacity Act 2005, D restrains P if he *"uses, or threatens to use, force to secure the doing of an act which P resists, or restricts P's liberty of movement, whether or not P resists."*

Special provision is made for the application of those principles where an act is done which will restrict a person's liberty. Sections 5 and 6 of the MCA 2005 authorise a person (D) to restrict the liberty of movement of another person (P) in connection with his care or treatment, provided that:

- D takes reasonable steps to establish whether P has capacity in relation to that matter

- D reasonably believes that P lacks capacity in relation to that matter and that it will be in P's best interests for the act to be done

- D reasonably believes that it is necessary to restrict P's liberty of movement

- the restriction is a proportionate response to the likelihood of P suffering harm if the restriction was not imposed and the seriousness of that harm

Section 5 of the Mental Capacity Act 2005 provides protection against civil and criminal liability for certain acts done in connection with the care or treatment of P which would normally require consent. In short, D must take reasonable steps to establish whether P lacks capacity and must reasonably believe both that P lacks capacity and that it will be in P's best interests for the act to be done. This is not a substituted decision or substituted consent. It does not create any new powers of intervention, nor any new duties to act, nor does it exclude liability for negligence in doing the act. If the act is intended to restrain P, additional restrictions in Section 6 apply. Section 6 authorises restraint, including restrictions on the liberty of movement, where the restraint is necessary and is a proportionate response to the likelihood and seriousness of the potential harm.

In relation to care plans where the use of restraint is prescribed, the MCA Code of Practice provides that:

"The preparation of a care plan should always include an assessment of the person's capacity to consent to the actions covered by the care plan, and confirm that those actions are agreed to be in the person's best interests. Healthcare and social care staff may then be able to assume that any actions they take under the care plan are in the person's best interests, and therefore receive protection from liability under Section 5. But a person's capacity and best interests must still be reviewed regularly."
(Paragraph 6.24)

Case law examples on restraint and seclusion and deprivation of liberty

Looking back over the past decade it is clear that there have always been significant concerns about the use of restraint or other restrictive measures, which may result in an individual being deprived of their liberty. What follows is a review of the relevant cases that may guide the reader to determine what type of restraints amount to a deprivation of liberty.

Box 1

In the case of *Surrey CC v MB* [2007] EWHC 3085 (Fam), the respondent (*M*) was a man with autism, behavioural problems and learning difficulties who was living in the community. *M* was considered to lack the relevant capacity to make decisions as to his residence, care and treatment.

The applicant considered it to be in *M*'s best interests for him to be transferred to an assessment and treatment unit, but *M* refused to move as he wanted to remain in the community. The clinicians caring for *M* considered that he suffered from a mental disorder for the purposes of the Mental Health Act 1983 Section 2, however they would not support or apply for his detention under the Act and therefore this matter was brought before the court to determine:

- whether the case should be transferred to the Court of Protection for declarations

- whether the power granted to the court by the Mental Capacity Act 2005 Section 15(1)(c) enabled it to make a declaration which required *M* to go to the unit and be detained there, which ultimately deprived *M* of his liberty

- whether the court should exercise that power if the same result could be achieved under the 1983 Act

The court found that there was significant interplay between Section 15 of the 2005 Act and the provisions of the 1983 Act, which warranted a transfer of the proceedings to the Court of Protection. The provisions of Section 15(1)(c) of the Mental Capacity Act 2005 allowed the court to make a declaration, which compelled *M* to go to the unit and be detained there against his wishes. When considering the implications of the European Convention on Human Rights 1950 Article 5, the court considered that there would be no deprivation if:

- *M* was incapable of making a decision about going to the unit himself

- being required to remain in the unit would be in his best interests

- the court had declared it to be in his best interests to be compelled to remain there by the use of reasonable and proportionate measures

- there was a mechanism for review of his capacity and best interest in that regard

In this case, a choice was to be made between placement in the community and placement in the unit and balancing all factors, it was held that it would be in *M*'s best interests to reside at the unit and a declaration to this effect was therefore made with the situation to be supervised and a review to take place as soon as was reasonably practicable.

In these cases, the court's discretion is to be exercised judicially and possible alternatives should always be considered before any declarations are made which result in an individual being deprived of their liberty. Decision makers are granted the power under Section 5 and Section 6 of the Mental Capacity Act 2005 to make best interest decisions without going to court which presents a clear indication that an application under the MCA 2005 should not be taken as a first step but rather, it should be considered when other alternatives have not been available or possible.

Box 2

In *LBH v GP* (2010) 13 C.C.L. Rep. 171, G was a 29-year-old man who had a learning disability and resided with his mother in a hostel for homeless people. Each day, G was left alone whilst his mother went to work and he would spend his whole day sitting alone in one room without appropriate care and attention being provided to him. G was considered to be neglected in this environment and his health was deteriorating as a result. The applicant local authority applied to the court for declarations relating to the care arrangements for G in light of his mother's unwillingness to engage with the local authority and her continued aggression towards local authority staff.

In the circumstances and in view of the need to remove G from the situation, it was declared lawful for the local authority, with the assistance of the police, to enter the accommodation where G was living and to use a minimum degree of restraint and force to effect his transfer to a care home.

Given the expert findings in relation to the neglect that he had suffered whilst at the hostel and his lack of capacity to make decisions about the proceedings along with his demonstrated improvement at the care home and his own desire not to return to the hostel, the court considered that there was no deprivation of liberty in the arrangements made and it was clearly in G's best interests to remain at the care home in the circumstances.

Guidance was issued by the court in this case and related to the management of situations where an individual with a disability or someone lacking capacity is required to be removed from a specific care setting with the help of local authority staff and/or the police. The court stated that certain steps should be taken in these circumstances as follows:

- The relevant public body should, in advance of any application to the court for authorisation to remove a person, discuss and if possible agree the way in which the removal will be effected and the extent to which restraint or force might be required and the nature of such restraint or force.

- Information about the way in which the removal is to be effected should be provided to the court and the litigation friend before the court authorises such removal.

- If there is disagreement about how removal should be effected, the court should ensure that any authorisation for removal is given on a fully informed basis.

It is clear that restraint and force should only be used in limited circumstances where it is a requirement to ensure a person's safety and in their best interests as well as being the least restrictive option available.

Box 3

In the later case of *GJ, NJ and BJ (Incapacitated Adults)* [2008] EWHC 1097 (Fam) the court was required to determine the appropriate procedural safeguards to be implemented in situations where an individual without the relevant capacity was put in a placement which essentially involved the deprivation of his liberty. In the circumstances, Mr Justice Munby declared, in Paragraph 8 of the judgement, it to be lawful and in GJ's best interests to continue to reside in a placement where *"specified reasonable and proportionate measures were to be taken to prevent B [GJ] from leaving, prevent a risk of harm from arising and to regulate contact with other people."*

It is clear that where a person lacks capacity, and is subject to a deprivation of liberty and the use of restraint and/or reasonable force, there are significant requirements placed on the body who is implementing such restraint, force or deprivation. The court in this case confirmed that regular reviews ought to take place in order to comply with the European Convention on Human Rights 1950, Article 5(4). Regular evidence also needs to be sought to confirm that such arrangements are in the person's best interests.

Box 4

Following on from the above is the case of *Dorset CC v EH* [2009] EWHC 784 (Fam) which relates to *E* who was an elderly lady who was suffering from Alzheimer's which is a progressive condition. *E* lived alone and it was accepted that she lacked the capacity to make decisions as to where she should live and the care and treatment she should receive.

The applicant local authority had tried to implement support to help *E* manage within her own home during the two years prior to an application being made to the court. Unfortunately, the support had not been entirely successful and the local authority considered *E* to be at significant risk of harm to herself.

Despite objections from the Official Solicitor who considered that *E* should live in her own home where her autonomy could be maintained, the local authority sought declarations from the court that *E* lacked the capacity to make decisions about where she should live, that it was in her best interests for her to reside in a care home and that it was lawful for the local authority to use reasonable and proportionate measures to prevent her from leaving the secure care home.

Mr Justice Parker stated, in Paragraph 125, *"The court's protective jurisdiction exercisable in respect of a person who lacks capacity is subject to checks and safeguards in the Act, and governed by the overriding principles in the convention."* Section 122 of the judgement goes on to say, *"There is a checklist for the court to consider, namely whether it is in the best interests of the relevant person to be deprived of their liberty, whether it is necessary… and whether the deprivation of liberty is a proportionate response to the likelihood of the person suffering harm and the seriousness of that harm."*

The court considered that it had to carry out a balance sheet exercise of the pros and cons involved in depriving *E* of her liberty and putting restrictions and restraint upon her. In this case, it was evident that the benefits out-weighed the risks and it was therefore considered to be in *E*'s best interests for her to move to a secure home to prevent the risk of harm to herself. Mr Justice Parker in his concluding remarks stated, Paragraph 141, *"In principle, if E will not move to the care home voluntarily, then she will have to be moved under restraint. If such a declaration is necessary the applicant ought by then to know what the specific problems are likely to be and to put forward more detailed proposals addressing the measures likely to be necessary."*

Again, it is evident that where a body wishes to subject a person to restraint and/or a deprivation of their liberty, the court must consider and follow the checks and safeguards in the Act which are designed to prevent unnecessary restraint being placed on vulnerable incapacitated individuals.

Box 5

In the case of *DCC V KH (unreported)* [2009] COP 11729380, *KH* was a young man who was subject to an order that it was in his best interests to reside at a care home due to his family situation. *KH* was considered to lack the capacity to decide where he should live and who he should have contact with. Following contact sessions with his mother who lived over 100 miles away from the care home, *KH* had expressed a wish not to return to the care home and demonstrated extremely challenging behaviour in which he would assault care home staff as a result.

The local authority sought a declaration confirming that it could use a reasonable degree of force to ensure *KH* returned to the care home after contact sessions with his mother. Relying on the Deprivation of Liberty Safeguards Code of Practice, Paragraph 2.14 and 2.15, the local authority argued that the standard authorisation that was in place in relation to *KH*'s residence at the care home did not adequately protect them in the situation where restraint may need to be used.

At Paragraph 10 of his judgement, District Judge O'Regan held that a *"standard authorisation when in force is said to be sufficient protection for the return of a person to a care home or hospital, where the deprivation of liberty has been authorised, without any additional authority."* (Mental Health Law Online article – *DCC v KH* 2009 COP 11729380)

The court considered that the Deprivation of Liberty Safeguards Code of Practice was only to be used when addressing a situation where no standard authorisation was yet in force and in this case the use of reasonable force to ensure *KH*'s return to the care home was permitted by the standard authorisation.

Box 6

In 2010 in the Court of Protection the following landmark case was heard, *G v E* [2010] EWHC 621 (Fam). *E* was a 19-year-old man who suffered from a rare and complex condition known as tuberous sclerosis as well as learning difficulties. *E*'s development was slow and he was assessed as cognitively equivalent to a 2-year-old child. *E* was placed with a foster carer in 1995 on a temporary basis, but this became permanent and the same carer continued to support and care for *E* as he transitioned into adulthood.

Over time, *E*'s behaviour became more challenging and as he progressed into adulthood there were fears that *E*'s foster carer may be applying inappropriate physical restraint to him. The local authority placed *E* in an emergency respite unit whilst the matter was investigated and following an attack on staff he was later moved to a residential setting for adults with special needs. *E*'s sister applied to the court to determine:

- whether *E* had the capacity to decide where he should live

- whether the local authority had unlawfully detained *E* in breach of the European Convention on Human Rights ECHR 1950 Article 5

- whether the local authority had breached *E*'s right to a home or family life pursuant to Article 8 of the European Convention on Human Rights ECHR 1950

- whether it was in *E*'s best interests to live in a residential care home or return to his foster carer

Mr Justice Baker held that *E* lacked capacity to make decisions about where he should live. He also considered that the staff at the residential unit exercised complete control over the entirety of *E*'s care including his treatment, contacts and residence and he was therefore being deprived of his liberty under Article 5 of the European Convention on Human Rights ECHR 1950. No standard authorisation had been obtained by the local authority pursuant to schedule A1 of the Mental Capacity Act 2005 as is required in circumstances where an individual is being deprived of their liberty.

The court also found that *E*'s right to a home and family life under Article 8 of the ECHR had been infringed due to a lack of consideration by the local authority of *E*'s family life with his foster carer. It was stated in Mr Justice Baker's judgement that *E*'s foster carer had provided a high standard of care to *E* and had a great deal of insight relating to his needs, save for some concerns raised by *E*'s school in relation to mistreatment by *E*'s foster carer.

Despite the existence of a clear deprivation of liberty and infringements of the European Convention on Human Rights 1950, Mr Justice Baker concluded that *"when the principal benefits of returning E to F were balanced against the disadvantages, it can be concluded that E's best interests required him to remain at the residential unit."*

Interestingly, this case went to appeal on 16 July 2010 for the court to consider whether Article 5 of the European Convention on Human Rights 1950 places specific threshold conditions which have to be satisfied before a person who lacks capacity can be detained in his or her best interests under the Mental Capacity Act 2005. Mr Justice Baker had confirmed in his judgement that there was no threshold for an order under Section 16 in order to deprive someone of his liberty, save that the individual lacks the relevant capacity. Sir Nicholas Wall held on appeal, *G v E* [2010] EWCA Civ 822, Paragraph 58,

"We do not think that ECHR Article 5 imposes any threshold conditions which have to be satisfied before a best interests assessment under DOLS can be carried out."

The appeal was dismissed.

Box 7

In *A Local Authority v A and another* [2010] EWHC 978 (Fam), *A* and *C* were young people with Smith Magenis Syndrome, a rare genetic disorder which resulted in physical and verbal aggression, self harm, destructive behaviour and sleep disturbance. Both young people, who were over the age of 16 years of age, lived at home with their parents and as a result of their behaviour, were confined and locked in their bedrooms each night. This was considered to be the least restrictive option to ensure the safety of both children. Both young people were permitted to leave the room as soon as they knocked on the door or shouted for assistance.

Although the local authority and experts were supportive of this approach as the best way to ensure that A and C were safe at night, concerns were raised by the local authority that they would be in breach of their positive obligations under Article 5 of ECHR if it failed to prevent the apparent deprivation of liberty or to seek the court's approval to continue with such an approach.

The court had to consider both the objective and subjective test when looking at whether A and C were deprived of their liberty as follows:

- Were A and C being confined in a particularly restrictive space for a not negligible amount of time, having regard to the type, duration, effects and manner of implementation of the restrictions (the objective element)?

- Did A and C validly consent to their confinement (the subjective element)?

Mr Justice Munby agreed that both A and C lacked the capacity to consent to the restrictions they had been subjected to and therefore the local authority's positive obligations would be engaged in these circumstances. It was stated, in Paragraph 66, that whatever a local authority's positive obligations might be, they did not furnish it with *"any power to regulate, control, compel, restrain, confine or coerce. They are concerned with the provision of services and support."*

In relation to the objective element of these considerations, Mr Justice Munby confirmed, in Paragraph 115, that *"in my judgment, the loving, caring, regime in each of these family homes – a reasonable, proportionate and entirely appropriate regime implemented by devoted parents in the context of a loving family relationship and with the single view to the welfare, happiness and best interests of A and C respectively – falls significantly short of anything that would engage Article 5."*

It is interesting to see that this case turns on the issue of care provided by family members and it appears from the judgement of Mr Justice Munby that in these circumstances, strong evidence will be required in order to demonstrate that there is a deprivation of liberty in circumstances where a family member is providing care in what is seemingly a loving family context. In any other private care setting, it is likely that this would amount to a deprivation of liberty requiring standard authorisation. This raises the issue of when care provided by a family member is likely to meet the threshold to amount to a deprivation of liberty.

Box 8

In contrast to the previous case, Mr Justice Baker, in *BB v AM* [2010]
EWHC 1916 (Fam), was concerned with a 31-year-old Bangladeshi
woman who was diagnosed with schizoaffective disorder and learning
difficulties. *B* lived with her parents until the local authority removed
her and placed her in a hospital setting following reports that *B* was
being assaulted by her parents at home. Following admission into
hospital, *B* was subject to sedation and staff exercised complete
control over her care. The court was requested to consider whether
the criteria in Sections 2 or 3 of the Mental Health Act were met in
B's case, therefore rendering her ineligible to be deprived of her liberty.
The court found that *B* was not detainable under the Mental Health
Act and therefore she was not eligible to be deprived of her liberty.

Mr Justice Baker held at Paragraph 28 of his judgement that
*"It is important, and the Deprivation of Liberty Safeguards Code of Practice
reminds me, to consider all points cumulatively rather than in isolation."*
In considering the circumstances of this case, Mr Justice Baker held
at Paragraph 32 of his judgement *"To my mind, having regard to all the
factors identified in the DOLS Code of Practice and the circumstances of B's
current accommodation at C Hospital as set out in the evidence before me, I
conclude that she is being deprived of her liberty. She is away from her family,
in an institution under sedation in circumstances in which her contact with the
outside world is strictly controlled, her capacity to have free access to her family
is limited, now by court order and her movements under the strict control and
supervision of hospital staff. Taking these factors altogether, the cumulative
effect in my judgment is that B is currently being deprived of her liberty."*

Box 9

This case importantly confirms the approach taken by Mr Justice Charles to the interaction of the Mental Health Act 1983 and the Mental Capacity Act 2005 in *GJ v The Foundation Trust and Ors* [2009] EWHC 2972 (Fam) and also for the clarification regarding the approach to be taken to assessments of the deprivation of liberty. In *GJ v The Foundation Trust and Ors* [2009] EWHC 2972 (Fam), Charles J provided useful guidance on the interplay between the Mental Capacity Act 2005 and Mental Health Act 1983, in particular at Paragraphs 45 which stated:
"In my judgment, the deeming provisions alone, and together with that view on assessments, are strong pointers in favour if the conclusions that (a) the MHA 1983 is to have primacy when it applies, and (b) the medical practitioners referred to in Sections 2 and 3 of the MHA 1983 cannot pick and choose between the two statutory regimes as they think fit having regard to general considerations (eg the preservation or promotion of a therapeutic relationship with P) that they consider render one regime preferable to the other."

Box 10

The comments made by Mr Justice Baker as to the need for consistency of approach is welcome although does, again, raise the stark issue of the difficulty of dissemination of judgments. Somewhat more troubling, perhaps, is the indication that the courts will take a robust approach to determinations of deprivation of liberty questions on an interim basis. Whilst limited judicial resources are available as mentioned by the Court of Appeal in *G v E* [2010] EWCA Civ 822, it means that this is a reality, in many cases. An interim conclusion as to whether or not a situation constitutes a deprivation of liberty is likely to hold sway for many months, with significant consequences in terms of the obligations upon the relevant local authority or health or social care provider to review the position.

It is clear from the above cases that where there is the use of restraint, confinement or restrictions on ones freedom in a private care setting, a declaration from the court should be sought and is likely to confirm that the incapacitated individual is subject to a deprivation of their liberty.

Box 11

The case of *RK* [2010] EWHC 3355 (COP) (Fam) concerns the placement of *RK* in a care home by the local authority under Section 20 Children Act (CA) 1989 after her family became unable to care for her at home. *RK* was a 17½-year-old woman who had been diagnosed with autism, attention deficit hyperactivity disorder, severe learning disability and epilepsy, and displayed aggressive and self harming behaviours. The issue for the court was whether *RK* was deprived of her liberty in the care home placement. If she was, then being under 18, the Deprivation of Liberty Safeguard regime would not apply, and the local authority would have to apply to the court for declarations authorising the placement, with the consequent reviews.

Mr Justice Moyston held that there was no deprivation of liberty, either on the facts, or as a matter of law. He held that where a child is placed under Section 20 CA 1989 and the parents have a right under Section 20(8) CA 1989 to refuse consent to the placement, there can be no deprivation of liberty. Any restriction on *RK*'s freedom was the result of *RK*'s parents exercising parental responsibility by consenting to the placement, and thus the 'subjective' limb of the test for a deprivation of liberty could not be met. Nor was the objective test met, according to the judge, because *RK*'s care came nowhere near involving depriving her of her liberty. *RK* lived at the residential placement from Monday to Friday and attended school each day. She returned to her parent's home every weekend. While at the placement, she was allowed unrestricted contact with her parents, and was subject to close supervision at all times, but was apparently not restrained or subject to a particularly strict behavioural management regime. The door to the placement was not locked, although if *RK* had tried to leave, she would have been brought back.

In response to a submission that these arrangements amounted to confinement because they restricted *RK*'s autonomy, the judge said *"I am not sure that the notion of autonomy is meaningful for a person in RK's position."* He concluded: *"I find it impossible to say, quite apart from Section 20(8) Children Act 1989 that these factual circumstances amount to a 'deprivation of liberty'. Indeed it is an abuse of language to suggest it.*

To suggest that taking steps to prevent RK attacking others amounts to 'restraint' signifying confinement is untenable. Equally, to suggest that the petty sanctions I have identified signifies confinement is untenable. The supervision that is supplied is understandably necessary to keep RK safe and to discharge the duty of care. The same is true of the need to ensure that RK takes her medicine. None of these things whether taken individually or collectively comes remotely close to crossing the line marked deprivation of liberty."

Further, the local authority was not detaining *RK* under any 'formal powers', as would be the case if, for example, a care order was in place. *RK*'s parents could have removed her from the placement if they chose to withdraw their consent to it. If *RK*'s parents have decided not to remove her from the placement, the judge found it difficult to see how the state could be said to be responsible for her detention.

This decision seems to represent part of a growing unwillingness on the part of the High Court to recognise deprivations of liberty on the objective test. One is reminded of the submission on behalf of the government in the case of *HL v United Kingdom* [2005] 40 EHRR 32 (Bournewood case) when it reached the ECtHR that *HL* had not been deprived of his liberty, because if he was, then so were most residents of care homes and hospitals in England. The courts seem keen to ensure that that prediction is not fulfilled, even though *HL* was indeed found to have been deprived of his liberty.

The Judge's comment about autonomy not being a meaningful concept for someone in *RK*'s position is likely to raise concerns amongst those who work towards achieving greater independence for adults and young people with learning disabilities. Although *RK* may not achieve the sort of autonomy someone without her disabilities might enjoy, there are many ways in which her autonomy can be promoted, and she can be supported to direct the course of her life, for example in relation to expressing preferences and making choices about day to day or immediate matters.

Box 12

In the Court of Appeal case of *Surrey CC v CA* [2011] EWCA Civ 190, *P* and *Q* were aged 19 and 18 respectively and both were assessed as having the cognitive abilities of children aged between 2 and 4 years old. Both individuals were subject to care orders following their treatment within the family home which included excessive physical chastisement, neglect and deprivation. The Official Solicitor on behalf of *P* and *Q* unsuccessfully brought the appeal against the declaration that the care arrangements did not amount to a deprivation of liberty.

Factors taken into consideration in this case in order to determine whether there had been a deprivation of liberty were as follows:

- whether objections to the arrangements had been made
- whether drugs which might suppress the expression of objections had been used
- the normality of the living arrangements for *P* and *Q*
- the opportunities available for leaving the place of residence for the purposes of recreation, education and social contact

The Court of Appeal produced a list of factors which had been established in both cases and which demonstrated that there was no deprivation of liberty in this case:

- Both *P* and *Q* were not free to leave their respective accommodation.
- They did not object to the arrangements made for them.
- They did not seek to leave and therefore did not have to be restrained from leaving their accommodation.
- They were not under close confinement within their accommodation.
- They were taken out each day to the unit of further education.
- They were taken on regular outings and had regular outside contact with family members.

In the circumstances and although restraint was sometimes required in relation to Q's physical outbursts, the Court of Appeal held that the arrangements made did not amount to a deprivation of liberty so as to engage their rights under Article 5, European Convention on Human Rights 1950.

It appears that where there are no significant objections to the care arrangements put in place and no restraint being used in order to enforce the arrangements, the court has tended to consider that the placement does not amount to a deprivation of liberty as the individual concerned has not requested or made attempt to leave or object to the care arrangements.

Box 13

Another significant case in relation to the use of restraint and seclusion is the Court of Protection case of *A Local Authority v C* [2011] EWHC 1539 (Admin), which involved *C* who was an 18-year-old man with severe autism and profound learning disabilities which resulted in extremely challenging behaviour.

C's behaviour was suggested by the care provider to be uncontrollable and as a result, this was largely managed by the use of a padded blue room in which *C* was secluded when he exhibited challenging behaviours such as defecating, smearing and eating and drinking his own faeces and urine, aggression and stripping naked. He was not permitted to leave the blue room when he exhibited such behaviours and the room had a secure door and window so that carers were aware of how *C* was behaving when in the room.

The court was required to consider a number of issues and most significantly was the good practice being adopted in relation to *C*'s nakedness, to the use of seclusion and restraint and in particular the use and impact that the blue room had on *C*. In considering the latter, the court was tasked with consideration of whether *C* was being subject to inhuman and degrading treatment and also whether his right to liberty and respect for his private life had been infringed.

When considering the issues, Mr Justice Ryder found that of critical importance was the fact that as the Deprivation of Liberty Safeguards Code of Practice and Schedule A1 of the Mental Capacity Act 2005 did apply to *C*, an application should have been made to the Court of Protection before any deprivation of liberty occurred. Unfortunately, until the date that this case came before the court, there had been no lawful authority to deprive *C* of his liberty.

When considering the lawfulness of any seclusion, the court made reference to the Department of Health's *Guidance for Restrictive Physical Interventions: How to provide safe services for people with learning disabilities and autistic spectrum disorder* (2002) and the Northern Ireland Human Rights Working Group on Restraint and Seclusion document, *Guidance on Restraint and Seclusion in Health and Personal Social Services* (DHPSSNI, 2005). The court noted that if the blue room was to be used as a method of managing *C*'s aggressive behaviour, the school had to be clear that such seclusion was only being used for as long as was necessary and proportionate and that it was the least restrictive option. Mr Justice Ryder confirmed, in Paragraph 108, that an *"intervention and prevention plan for the use of the blue room and a document advising upon the management of C's nakedness is to be agreed."* The court confirmed that seclusion was not to be used solely for the reason of nakedness, or as a punishment to manage *C*'s behaviour or on the basis that *C* was self harming. Mr Justice Ryder went on to conclude in Paragraph 121 that *"As a consequence of the findings, decisions and approvals made by the court detailed orders and declarations under the Mental Capacity Act 2005 have been made providing for C's interim placement at the school but under very clearly defined procedures and constraints, in particular, concerning his seclusion. His liberty may be deprived in very limited circumstances and only with the authority of this court."*

It is clear that the decision made in this case will have wider implications for children's homes and residential schools who care for young people with challenging behaviours. This case confirms that in order to deprive a young person of their liberty and implement such restrictions and restraint on them, an application to the court for authority to engage in such action will be required prior to such action being taken. This case highlights the seriousness of the issues relating to young people and deprivation of liberty and strengthens the position that an individual who lacks capacity should not be deprived of their liberty save for in the most exceptional circumstances where it is considered to be in that person's best interests.

Box 14

Perhaps the most significant recent case in relation to the use of restraint on individuals who lack capacity is the Court of Appeal case of *Cheshire West and Chester Council v P* [2011] EWCA Civ 1257 ('*the Cheshire West case*') which concerned *P* who was a man with cerebral palsy and Down syndrome. As a result of his disabilities, *P* required substantial supervision and a high level of care on a day to day basis. *P* exhibited extremely challenging behaviour including self harm, aggression and pulling apart his continence pads and putting these into his mouth. When *P* demonstrated such behaviours, he was subject to physical restraint by at least two staff members by way of them inserting their fingers into his mouth in order to remove such items. In addition to the above intervention, *P* would often wear a body suit which was designed to prevent him from gaining access to his continence pads.

Mr Justice Baker found that *P* was being deprived of his liberty through the use of restraint by members of staff who effectively had complete control of his care and movement. The appeal was allowed on the basis that in the first instance, consideration had not been paid to the relative normality of *P*'s situation as was confirmed in the case of Paragraph 28–29, Mr Justice Wilson's judgement *Surrey CC v CA* [2011] EWCA Civ 190. When looking at the comparator for *P* in this situation, Mr Justice Munby confirmed that *P* should be compared *"not with the previous life led by X (nor with some future life that X might lead), nor with the life of the able-bodied man or woman on the Clapham omnibus, but with the kind of lives that people like X would normally expect to lead. The comparator, in other words, is an adult of similar age with the same capabilities as X, affected by the same condition or suffering the same inherent mental and physical disabilities and limitations as X."*
Paragraph 97 of Mr Justice Munby's judgement.

In the circumstances of *P*'s case, he was considered to be leading a life which was similar to his relevant comparator and regardless of the care setting; an individual with *P*'s disabilities and behaviours would be subject to similar restrictions and interventions in order to maintain their general health and wellbeing. The appeal was granted and the court held that the restraint and intervention placed on *P* did not amount to a deprivation of liberty for the purposes of Article 5 of the European Convention on Human Rights 1950.

The result of this case has and is likely to cause further controversy and comment as it allows the court to consider the normality of one individual based on the similarities he may have with another individual with similar disabilities and therefore focuses on objectivity rather than subjectivity when looking at whether an individual who lacks capacity is deprived of their liberty. It appears that the judgement may have the ultimate affect of restricting the availability of deprivation of liberty safeguards to many vulnerable adults in care settings, which seemingly detracts from the fundamental position of protecting individuals in these circumstances.

This case was subject to appeal at the Supreme Court, [2014] UKSC 19 where Lady Hale reinforced the importance of the applicability of human rights to people with a disability:

"In my view, it is axiomatic that people with disabilities, both mental and physical, have the same human rights as the rest of the human race. It may be that those rights have sometimes to be limited or restricted because of their disabilities, but the starting point should be the same as that for everyone else. This flows inexorably from the universal character of human rights, founded on the inherent dignity of all human beings, and is confirmed in the United Nations Convention on the Rights of Persons with Disabilities. Far from disability entitling the state to deny such people human rights, rather it places upon the state (and upon others) the duty to make reasonable accommodation to cater for the special needs of those with disabilities.

Those rights include the right to physical liberty, which is guaranteed by Article 5 of the European Convention. This is not a right to do or to go where one pleases. It is a more focused right, not to be deprived of that physical liberty. But, as it seems to me, what it means to be deprived of liberty must be the same for everyone, whether or not they have physical or mental disabilities. If it would be a deprivation of my liberty to be obliged to live in a particular place, subject to constant monitoring and control, only allowed out with close supervision, and unable to move away without permission even if such an opportunity became available, then it must also be a deprivation of the liberty of a disabled person. The fact that living arrangements are comfortable, and indeed make my life as enjoyable as it could possibly be, should make no difference. A gilded cage is still a cage."

Lady Hale considered the existing Strasbourg case law and agreed that the classic test in *Guzzardi v Italy* (1980) 3 EHRR 333 is common in all the ECtHR cases: ie, the starting point is the 'concrete situation of the individual', and then one must always 'take account of a whole range of criteria such as the type, duration, effects and manner of implementation of the measures in question.' At Paragraph 48 of the judgment she went on to say that:

"But these cases are not about the distinction between a restriction on freedom of movement and the deprivation of liberty. P, MIG and MEG are, for perfectly understandable reasons, not free to go anywhere without permission and close supervision. So what are the particular features of their 'concrete situation' on which we need to focus."

Box 14

In *ZH v Commissioner of Police for the Metropolis* [2012] EWHC 604, Z was a 19-year-old man who suffered from severe autism and epilepsy. On a school visit to a local swimming pool, Z became fixated on the water and stood at the edge of the pool for a long period of time without moving. Z's carers knew that Z was averse to being touched and believed that if they did this, Z would jump into the pool. Z's carers tried to entice Z away from the pool by talking to him and offering him sweets and reassurance but this was not proving successful.

The pool manager became frustrated with the situation and called the police. On arrival, the police spoke to the carers and were aware that Z was afraid of being touched and would not react well if they touched him. The officers' approach was that Z was at risk of harm to himself and others and they therefore needed to take control of the situation. One of the officers touched *Z* on his back and at that point, he jumped into the pool. *Z* was subsequently lifted from the pool some 5-10 minutes later and was then restrained with the use of handcuffs and leg restraints by five officers as he continued to struggle and wrestle free. *Z* was finally released when a carer managed to calm him down.

Amongst others, one of the critical questions for the court was whether the commissioner was liable for depriving *Z* of his liberty under Article 5, European Convention on Human Rights 1950. Sir Robert Nelson considered the issue of force in great detail and at Paragraph 36 of his judgement states *"Section 6(2) Mental Capacity Act 2005 adds the requirement where restraint is carried out, that the defendant reasonably believes it is necessary to do the act in order to prevent harm to the person lacking capacity, and Section 6(3) requires that the act is a proportionate response to the likelihood of the person lacking capacity suffering harm, and the seriousness of that harm. The reasonable belief under both Section 5 and Section 6 has to be held when the act is being performed."*

The court went on to suggest that a clear distinction must be made between a deprivation of liberty and a restriction of movement. In this case, the defendant relied upon the use of restraint as being lawful and therefore not in contravention of Article 5 of the ECHR. The defendant commissioner also sought to rely on the dicta arising from Baroness Hale's judgement in the case of *Secretary of State for the Home Department v JJ* [2007] 3 WLR 642 where it was stated *"It also appears that restrictions designed, at least in part, for the benefit of the person concerned are less likely to be considered a deprivation of liberty than restrictions designed for the protection of society."*

When considering all the factors in this case in relation to the use of restraint and whether it was reasonable in the circumstances and the least restrictive option available, Sir Robert Nelson held *"The nature and duration of the restraint lead me to the conclusion that there was a deprivation of liberty, not merely a restriction on movement on the facts of this case… actions of the police were in general well intentioned but they involved the application of forcible restraint for a significant period of time of an autistic epileptic young man when such restraint was in the circumstances hasty, ill-informed and damaging to Z."*

The result of this case seems to highlight the importance of a public body ensuring that all possible alternatives have been considered before restraint is used as it is only in the most exceptional of circumstances where restraint will be accepted as necessary, reasonable and proportionate and therefore not amounting to a deprivation of liberty in accordance with Section 5 and 6 Mental Capacity Act 2005.

Having regard to the above, it can occasionally be difficult to extract the relevant principles from case law, especially in the context of what amounts to a deprivation of liberty. For clarity, and in drawing the threads together, the following assertions are suggested guiding principles summarising the above.

First, in determining whether there is a deprivation of liberty within the meaning of Article 5 ECHR, three conditions must be satisfied:

1. An objective element of a person's confinement in a particular restricted space for a not negligible time.

2. A subjective element, namely that the person has not validly consented to the confinement in question and such consent can only be valid if the person has capacity to give it.

3. The deprivation of liberty must be one for which the State is responsible.

Second, case law from the European Court of Human Rights, *Ashingdane v United Kingdom* (1985) 7 EHRR 528 Paragraph 41, tells us that the distinction between restrictions upon liberty and deprivations of liberty is one of degree or intensity rather than nature and substance and will therefore depend on criteria such as the type, duration, effects and manner of implementation of the measure. Those principles have been considered in the context of the sorts of decisions which are now made under the Mental Capacity Act 2005. Practitioners must be aware of the importance of striking a balance between using lawful restraint without such use resulting in the deprivation of a person's liberty.

Third, and fundamentally, the Supreme Court in the Cheshire West case clearly set out the **test** as to whether an individual is deprived of their liberty:

- whether the person is under continuous supervision and control

- not free to leave (in the sense of removing himself permanently in order to live where and with whom he chooses), see Paragraph 49 of the judgment

References

A Local Authority v A and another [2010] EWHC 978 (Fam)

A Local Authority v C [2011] EWHC 1539 (Admin)

A Local Authority v MA, NA and SA (by her children's guardian LJ) [2005] EWHC 2942 (Fam)

Ashingdane v United Kingdom (1985) 7 EHRR 528 at Paragraph 41

BB v AM [2010] EWHC 1916 (Fam)

Buck v Germany [2005] ECHR 41604/98

Cameron v Network Rail (Infrastructure Ltd) [2007] 1 WLR 163

Care Standards Act 2000. Available to download at www.legislation.gov.uk

Cheshire West and Chester Council v P [2011] EWCA Civ 1257, [2014] UKSC 19

Children Act 1989. Available to download at www.legislation.gov.uk

DCC v KH (unreported) [2009] COP 11729380 http://bit.ly/ViBZG9 [Accessed 26.6.14]

Department of Health (2006) *Bournewood Briefing Sheet*. London: DH

Department of Health (2014) *Positive and Proactive Care: Reducing the need for restrictive interventions*. London: DH

Department of Health and Department for Education and Skills (2002) *Guidance for Restrictive Physical Interventions: How to provide safe services for people with learning disabilities and autistic spectrum disorder*. London: DH

DHPSSNI (2005) *Guidance on Restraint and Seclusion in Health and Personal Social Services*. Belfast: DHPSSNI

Dorset CC v EH [2009] EWHC 784 (Fam)

G v E [2010] EWHC 621 (Fam)

G v E [2010] EWCA Civ 822

GJ v The Foundation Trust and Ors [2009] EWHC 2972 (Fam)

GJ, NJ and BJ (Incapacitated Adults) [2008] EWHC 1097 (Fam)

Guzzardi v Italy (1980) 3 EHRR 333

HL v United Kingdom [2005] 40 EHRR 32

Human Rights Act 1998. Available to download at www.legislation.gov.uk

JE v Surrey County Council [2006] EWHC 3459 (Fam)

Kent Pharmaceuticals Ltd v UK no 9355/03, 11 October 2005

Kjeldsen, Busk Madsen and Pedersen v Denmark (1976) 1 EHRR 711

LBH v GP (2010) 13 C.C.L. Rep. 171

London and Quadrant Housing Trust v R on the application of Weaver and the Equality and Human Rights Commission [2009] EWCA Civ 597

Lyon, CM and Pimor, A (2004) *Physical Interventions and the Law: Legal issues arising from the use of physical interventions in supporting children, young people and adults with learning disabilities and severe challenging behaviour*. Birmingham: BILD

Mental Capacity Act 2005. Available to download at www.legislation.gov.uk

Mental Health Act 1983. Available to download at www.legislation.gov.uk

National Assistance Act 1948. Available to download at www.legislation.gov.uk

Nelstrop, L et al (2006) A systematic review of the safety and effectiveness of restraint and seclusion as interventions for the short-term management of violence in adult psychiatric inpatient settings and emergency departments. *World Views on Evidence Based Nursing*, 3(1), 8–18

Paley, S (2009) Seclusion and time out: questioning and defining practice. In: Allen, D (ed) *Ethical Approaches to Physical Interventions. Volume II: Changing the agenda.* Birmingham: BILD

Pretty v United Kingdom (2002) 35 EHRR 1

R v Attorney General and Anor ex p. Countryside Alliance [2007] UKHL 52

R v Chief Constable of South Yorkshire Police ex p LS and Marper [2004] UKHL 39

R (AM) v SOSHD [2009] EWCA Civ 219

R (Animal Defenders International) v Secretary of State for Culture, Media and Sport [2008] UKHL 15

R (Baiai) v Secretary of State for the Home Department (Nos 1 and 2) [2007] EWCA Civ 478

R (Clift) v Secretary of State for the Home Department [2007] 1 AC 484 [27]-[28]

R (G) v Nottinghamshire Healthcare NHS Trust [2009] EWCA Civ 795 (CA)

R (James) v Secretary of State for Justice [2009] UKHL 22

R (L) (A Patient) v Secretary of State for the Home Department [2007] EWCA Civ 767

R (Malik) v Waltham Forest NHS Primary Care Trust [2007] 1 WLR 2092

R (on the application of Purdy) (Appellant) v Director of Public Prosecutions (Respondent) [2009] EWCA Civ 92

R (on the application of Purdy) (Appellant) v Director of Public Prosecutions (Respondent) [2009] UKHL 45

R (Pretty) v Director of Public Prosecutions (Secretary of State for the Home Department Intervening) [2002] 1 AC 800

R (RJM) v Secretary of State for Work and Pensions [2007] EWCA Civ 614

R (S) v Chief Constable of the South Yorkshire Police [2004] UKHL 39

R (Smith) v Oxfordshire Assistant Deputy Coroner [2009] EWCA Civ 441

R (Ullah) v Special Adjudicator [2004] UKHL 26

R (Wright) v Secretary of State for Health
[2007] EWCA Civ 999

RK [2010] EWHC 3355 (COP) (Fam)

SA (Vulnerable Adult with Capacity: Marriage)
[2005] EWHC 2942 (Fam)

Secretary of State for the Home
Department SSHD v JJ [2007] UKHL 45

Secretary of State for the Home
Department v JJ [2007] 3 WLR 642

Secretary of State for the Home
Department v E [2007] UKHL 47

Surrey CC v CA [2011] EWCA Civ 190

Surrey CC v MB [2007] EWHC 3085 (Fam)

Société Colas Est v France (2004) 39 EHRR 17

Wieser and Bicos Beteiligungen GMBH
v Austria [2007] ECHR 74336/01
(16 October 2007)

YL v Birmingham City Council [2007] UKHL 27

ZH v Commissioner of Police for the
Metropolis [2012] EWHC 604

Chapter 2

The importance of safeguarding rights and the role of legislation: the Australian perspective

Jeffrey Chan, Lynne Webber and Phillip French

Introduction

This chapter argues the case for strong legislative measures that articulate the human rights of people with a disability who are subject to or at risk of restrictive practices and which provide effective protection against the violation of these rights. It examines the development of legislation of this type in the Australian context, observing its broad characteristics and its strengths and limitations. Particular attention is given to the Victorian experience as the first state to enact legislation of this kind. While it is too early to draw firm conclusions about the success or otherwise of Australian legislative measures in protecting the human rights of people with a disability subject to restrictive practices, it is already clear that such legislation is capable of significant improvement. Additionally, it is also clear that legislative responses are necessary, but not by themselves sufficient, to achieve the sought for significant structural changes. Cross-sectoral and organisational strategies capable of impacting on organisational leadership, culture and practice are also required.

Human rights are a foundation for a contemporary and civilised society (Ramcharan, 2008; Ward and Stewart, 2008). The recognition, respect, protection and fulfilment of human rights are core international obligations of every civilised society, and one that is incorporated into all international human rights treaties (Ramcharan, 2008). However, despite these obligations, human rights violations continue in all parts of the world and these violations impact in aggravated ways on vulnerable population groups (Dimopoulos, 2010; Owens et al, 2009; Ramcharan, 2008). People with intellectual disability are one of those vulnerable groups of people whose fundamental human rights are most at risk (Dimopoulos, 2010; Owens et al, 2009). This risk is especially aggravated for people with intellectual disability and autism who present with behaviours of concern and are subject to the use of restrictive practices that may infringe on their human rights and dignity (Chan, French and Webber, 2011; Webber, McVilly and Chan, 2011; Sturmey, 2009).

The purpose of this chapter is not to establish the actual and potential harm that restrictive practices present to people with intellectual disability and autism. There is ample research evidence that establishes this harm and a growing research evidence to recommend alternatives to the use of restrictive practices (Chan et al, 2011; Chan, LeBel and Webber, 2012; Sturmey, 2009; Tsiouris, 2010; Tyrer et al, 2006; Webber, McVilly, Fester and Chan, 2011). This is the starting point, as is the direct applicability of the fundamental human rights and freedoms recognised or declared in the United Nations Convention on the Rights of Persons with Disabilities (CRPD) (United Nations, 2006) to people who are at risk of restrictive practices because of their behaviours of concern or offending behaviours. Protection and fulfilment of their human rights and dignity must be the primary objective of, and constraint on, clinical and social interventions with these groups (Chan et al, 2011; Chan, French, Hudson and Webber, 2011; Dimopoulos, 2010; French, Chan and Carracher, 2010; Webber et al, 2010).

The safeguarding of human rights is not an uncommon theme in international and national public policy discourse or in legislation dealing with persons with intellectual disability (Dimopoulos, 2010; Romijn and Frederiks, 2012). Legislative approaches do have their limitations. Romijn and Frederiks (2012) undertook a review of government legislation and regulations that are aimed to reduce restraint use in three countries (Netherlands, United Kingdom and Australia). They note that while these practices may be regulated, actual practice is not always in line with legislative policy. At least with respect to the State of Victoria in Australia this conclusion should not be adopted uncritically, as experience does suggest legislatively driven practice improvement (see the Office of the Senior Practitioner Annual Reports for the years 2008, 2009, 2010 and 2011).

Similarly, Keski-Valkama et al (2007) suggest that legislation itself may not be sufficient to safeguard the rights of people with intellectual disability subject to restrictive practices.

Nevertheless, it is argued that legislation is a critical starting point in the protection of the rights of people with a disability subject to restrictive practices and a necessary, though not sufficient, element of any structural response to the issue that is capable of penetrating the varying levels of organisational leadership, culture and practice. This chapter will argue the case for specific legislation that responds to the harm caused by restrictive practices and which protects the human rights of persons who are, or who are at risk of being, subject to restrictive practices. It will provide an overview and discussion of legislative responses to restrictive practices in three Australian states and review the Victorian model for protecting the rights of people with a disability subject to restrictive practices in particular. Finally, it will propose a good practice model for safeguarding the dignity and human rights of people with intellectual disability and autism who are at risk of being subjected to restrictive practices.

Why are ethics and legislation important in safeguarding rights

Human rights are applicable to all persons, in all contexts, at all times. However, there can be little debate that people with intellectual disability, especially those subject to restrictive practices, are prone to having their fundamental rights ignored and violated. Historically, people with a disability have been viewed as objects of treatment and this treatment has, in large part, been disassociated in theory and in practice with their underlying humanity. Nowhere is this more the case than it is with respect to the use of restrictive practices. Practices which have caused discomfort and pain, restricted the liberty and autonomy of the person, and those which have suppressed personality and consciousness have been widely used in disability service and mental health contexts (Chan et al, 2012).

In some cases, these practices may have been 'successful' in eliminating or suppressing a behaviour that placed that individual or someone else at risk, but in many other cases they have resulted in little change or have made things worse. Even where success in the elimination of problem behaviours has been achieved, sometimes it is appropriate to ask at what price for the individual this success has come.

In this respect, it is notable that the United Nations Special Rapporteur on Torture has recently drawn attention to the brutality and violence that may be associated with the use of a number of restrictive practices used frequently on persons with intellectual disability who engage in behaviours of concern, including chemical and physical restraint and seclusion, and has called for the reframing of these practices, at least in some circumstances, as violence, abuse and human rights violations (United Nations, 2008).

The CRPD, which was adopted by the United Nations General Assembly in December 2006 and which entered into force internationally in May 2008, encapsulates and mandates a paradigm shift away from a conception of persons with a disability as objects for treatment to their recognition as human rights bearers entitled to the enjoyment of equal dignity and rights with all other persons. In its articles, the CRPD addresses the central human rights concerns articulated by the international movement of persons with disabilities during the negotiation process. Not surprisingly, given the history of treatment of people with a disability in medical, mental health and disability service settings, no less than five of its articles (Articles 14 to 17 and 19) address protection from various forms of violence and abuse, including deprivation of liberty, compulsory (or forced) treatment and institutionalisation. The CRPD has, and will increasingly become a driver of disability related reform at the international and national levels including in relation to the use of restrictive practices.

All state parties that ratify (that is, agree to become legally bound by) the CRPD enter into a series of solemn obligations to give effect to the rights it enshrines. These obligations include the enactment of domestic legislation to give effect to the treaty and the repeal of legislative provisions that are inconsistent with the treaty (Article 4). This is especially important in the Australian context (as it is in many others) because ratification of an international treaty does not automatically incorporate the provisions of the treaty into domestic law. This only occurs where an Australian parliament enacts domestic legislation to give effect to the provisions of treaty.

Legislative action is only one of the obligations enumerated, but it is nevertheless of fundamental significance to CRPD implementation efforts. Certainly, a failure to take legislative action to implement CRPD rights domestically would be a strong basis for international criticism. This is because legislation is one of the most concrete and potent ways in which a state can signal its intention to actually comply with, rather than merely superficially espouse, human rights. Of course, much also depends upon the scope and content of any legislative provisions.

The developments reviewed in this chapter might be conceptualised as a 'second-wave' of legislative activity in the Australian context in relation to the regulation of restrictive practices. Generally speaking, the first wave concentrated on the enactment of guardianship legislation and the designation of people who are authorised to consent or refuse consent to the use of restrictive practices (although Victoria also established an independent review panel to oversee the use of these practices). The legislative assumption was that the individual's rights were protected because their guardian or a guardianship authority would not consent, or permit consent, to an abusive or unnecessary practice. There has been no systematic analysis of the success of guardianship legislation in protecting the rights of people subject to restrictive practices. However, it is a direct implication of the work undertaken by the Victorian Law Reform Commission and Justice Carter in Victoria and Queensland respectively (outlined below), which stimulated the second wave reforms in those states, that the guardianship approach has failed.

Although the second-wave Victorian legislation was developed and enacted prior to the CRPD's adoption and entry into force, it was nevertheless significantly influenced by human rights discourse, including that emanating from the CRPD treaty negotiations which commenced in 2001. Subsequent legislative developments in Australia have been very directly influenced by the human rights approach mandated by the CRPD. Of course, this is not to say that these Australian legislative developments are in all respects consistent with the CRPD. Indeed, particular legislative provisions are arguably incompatible with CRPD rights. Nevertheless, in key respects this legislation implements a human rights approach.

Legislation is not only important for its potential to recognise or make human rights operative in a domestic context. It is also normative. It establishes (or at least has the potential to establish) values and principles, objectives and standards which must be observed and around which administrative action must be organised. It can designate lawful and unlawful conduct, and create civil and criminal penalties for those persons that engage in unlawful conduct. In each of these respects, it is capable of creating organisational and individual behavioural change.

It is also structural in impact. It has the potential to designate roles and responsibilities for the doing of things (including by articulating the functions and powers of particular officers), to create key accountabilities, and to establish monitoring and review processes. In these respects, it has the potential to both centralise and decentralise administrative action. While we observe later in this chapter that legislative measures are insufficient in themselves to effectively protect the rights of persons subject to restrictive practices, it is difficult to imagine how such protection can be achieved in large, diffuse human service systems without it.

Finally (although not exhaustively so) legislation has the potential to establish the means by which people with a disability and their associates can enforce their rights. It can establish complaint mechanisms, review processes, and civil liability in relation to the unreasonable or unlawful use of restrictive practices. In this respect it can give genuine power to otherwise powerless individuals and assist in addressing the vast power imbalance that exists between the clinician and the system responsible for the administration of restrictive practices and the individual who is subjected to these practices.

Overview of the Australian experience in safeguarding the rights of people with disability subject to restrictive practices

In Australia, there are three states (Victoria, Queensland and Tasmania) that have enacted laws to safeguard the rights of people with intellectual disability who are subject to restrictive practices, and those who come into contact with the criminal justice system. At the time of writing this chapter, it is important to note that there is also a bill before the Northern Territory Parliament to amend the Territory's Disability Services Act to incorporate protections for people with intellectual disability who may be subject to restrictive practices and those adults who are viewed as requiring detention due to a significant risk to themselves and/or others (Northern Territory Bills, 2011). In South Australia, the Social Inclusion Board produced a document, *Strong Voices, a Blueprint to Enhance Life and Claim the Rights of People with Disability in South Australia (2012-2020)* that expressed similar concerns and interest in enhancing and protecting the rights of people with a disability, and one of the key issues highlighted is protecting those subject to restrictive practices (South Australian Social Inclusion Board, 2011). South Australia has also established a Senior Practitioner role similar to Victoria, however there is minimal information provided at the time of writing this chapter about the South Australian model.

Protecting the rights of people with a disability subject to restrictive practices is definitely a growing area of interest and concern in Australia. This overview will briefly discuss the contexts for the respective legislative protections in place in Victoria, Queensland and Tasmania, and will also discuss the similarities and differences in the legislative responses in these jurisdictions. It is not within the scope of this chapter to provide a detailed comparative overview or critique of the specific legal provisions and in any event, such an exercise may have limited value given the contextual differences between jurisdictions.

Victoria was the first Australian state to enact specific legislation to provide for the protection of the rights of people with a disability subject to restrictive interventions and compulsory treatment orders. Compulsory treatment orders are made in relation to those individuals who are diverted from the criminal justice system for the purpose of habilitation and social re-integration. Restrictive interventions are designated as chemical and mechanical restraints and seclusion (Disability Act 2006). In Victoria, the Law Reform Commission's report, *People with Intellectual Disabilities at Risk* (Victorian Law Reform Commission, 2003) highlighted concerns regarding the lack of protection for people who were subject to high levels of restrictive interventions and/or detention and prompted amendments to the existing disability services legislation to include a series of specific rights protections that will be briefly highlighted.

The intent of the Victorian legislation to protect rights is made clear in the purpose and objectives of the legislation as it reaffirms and strengthens the rights and responsibilities of people with a disability (Part 2, Division 5, s23–27; Part 7 and Part 8, Disability Act, 2006). The creation of the role of the Senior Practitioner was a specific recommendation of the Victorian Law Reform Commission to protect the rights of people with disability subject to restrictive interventions and compulsory treatment (Disability Act, 2006). Victorian disability services legislation applies to funded disability services including group homes, congregate care settings, respite services, day programmes, and facilities that provide care for individuals in contact with the criminal justice system.

There are several key legislative provisions that regulate and monitor the use of restrictive practices (Disability Act, 2006). For example, disability service providers have to apply to the chief executive of the government department responsible for the administration of disability services if they intend to use restrictive practices; the use of restrictive practices is only permissible when it is the least restrictive alternative and only when the behaviour presents a significant risk to self and/or others; a behaviour support plan is required for each person subject to such practices and the plan is to be authorised at the local level subject to the monitoring of the Senior Practitioner; and there is mandatory reporting to the Senior Practitioner for each episode of restrictive practice. The legislation provides further safeguards in that a person with a disability may at any time request a review of the behaviour support plan and the Public Advocate (an independent statutory role) may refer a matter to the Senior Practitioner to review the plan or take the matter further by referring it to the Victorian Civil and Administrative Tribunal (an independent body headed by a Supreme Court judge) (Disability Act, 2006). In addition, the law provides the Senior Practitioner with extensive functions and powers to ensure the legislation is complied with, such as by monitoring the use of restrictive practices, instigating investigations, audits and reviews in relation to an individual or a service; issuing directives to service providers to do or not do a thing (including to cease the use of a restrictive practice); impose further requirements to a use of restrictive interventions, developing and issuing guidelines and standards and initiating research (Part 7, s150; Disability Act, 2006).

In relation to individuals who may be subject to compulsory treatment orders, before such an order may be made by the Victorian Civil and Administrative Tribunal the disability service provider has to prepare a treatment plan which must be approved by the Senior Practitioner (Disability Act, 2006). The Senior Practitioner is also required to publish an annual report in relation to the performance of these legislative functions and related activities. The strategies established by the Senior Practitioner to prevent, reduce and/or safely eliminate restrictive practices are discussed later in this chapter.

The emphasis on safeguarding the rights of people subject to restrictive practices in Queensland was given prominence following an investigative report by Justice Carter (2006) commissioned by the Queensland government. Justice Carter discovered a significant level of poor practice and breaches of the rights of people with disability in Queensland. The report highlighted the vulnerability of people with intellectual disability and challenging behaviours, and who were subject to high levels of restrictive practices; and/or who were accommodated in mental health facilities. The report argued strongly that the human rights of the person must be the focus and driving force for change in the Queensland disability services system (Carter, 2006). Justice Carter delivered a series of recommendations for legislative change, including for the establishment of a system of independent regulation of the use of restrictive practices. He also strongly recommended the establishment of a centre of excellence to drive positive behaviour support implementation across the sector (Carter, 2006).

In response to the Carter recommendations, the Queensland government initiated the *Positive Futures* programme. The programme is a six-year $228 million government investment to promote good practice in positive behaviour support and protect the rights of adults with an intellectual disability or cognitive impairment who exhibit challenging behaviours. The programme included changes to the legislation; the establishment of the Centre of Excellence for Behaviour Support in partnership with the University of Queensland; the establishment of a Mental Health Assessment and Outreach Team; the establishment of a specialist response service to develop a positive behaviour support plan for adults with intellectual disability subject to restrictive practices; and, the development of specific accommodation models for individuals who exhibit challenging behaviours (Positive Futures, 2011).

The regulation of restrictive practices applies only to adults with an intellectual disability and covers containment and seclusion and chemical, mechanical and physical restraints for behavioural control of a person. (Disability Services and Other Legislation Amendment Act, 2008). Another restrictive practice defined in the Queensland legislation is restricted access to objects (Disability Services and Other Legislation Amendment Act, 2008). Similar to the Victorian legislation, the Queensland legislation constrains the use of restrictive practices to specific circumstances. It may only be used when it presents a significant risk to self and/or others; a multidisciplinary assessment and risk assessment must be undertaken; and any intervention must be based on the least restrictive principle (Disability Services and Other Legislation Amendment Act, 2008).

Unlike the Victorian legislation, the Queensland legislation does not provide for a senior clinical role in monitoring and investigating restrictive practices. Instead, there can be up to five different levels of approval or consent processes for each type of restrictive practice and there are different levels of review process for the restrictive practice (Disability Services and Other Legislation Amendment Act, 2008). The first level is for containment and seclusion where the Queensland Civil and Administrative Tribunal is the independent authority that provides approval and it is also responsible for reviewing the containment and seclusion of the adults with an intellectual or cognitive disability. An appointed guardian from the Office of the Adult Guardian (an independent statutory authority) may provide short-term approval for containment and seclusion and for other types of restrictive practices.

The next level is the requirement of an appointed guardian who may also provide approval for other types of restrictive practices, such as physical, chemical or mechanical restraints (Positive Futures, 2011). Another level is the requirement for short-term approvals of chemical, mechanical, physical restraints and restricting access if there is no guardian in the adult's life for restrictive practice matters. The Director-General of the Department of Communities (or delegate), in Queensland there is the role of *Individual Response Leader* (now called Director of Clinical Practice) as a type of clinical leader in most regions to provide clinical leadership in restrictive practices or exercise a particular function in the legislation, hold the delegation for short-term approval for some types of restrictive practices.

For respite and community access services, an informal decision maker if there is no guardian for restrictive practices can approve physical or mechanical restraint, and chemical restraint if it is for a fixed dose in respite services. An informal decision maker can approve restricting access (such as objects) if there is no guardian for restrictive practices. Given the complexity of approval levels, the Queensland government has called for a review of restrictive practices (Department of Communities, Child Safety and Disability Services, 2013).

Unlike the Victorian model, there is no provision in the Queensland legislation for monitoring of behaviour support plans and the reporting of the use of restrictive practices across the state. As such, there is no single repository in which such important data can be used and analysed to inform practice and policy changes. Unlike the Victorian model, there is also no provision for a person with a disability to request a review of the plan or the use of the restrictive practice once it had been consented to by the Office of the Adult Guardian.

In addition to the regulation of restrictive practices, Queensland has also legislated to safeguard the rights of adults with intellectual disability or cognitive impairment whose behaviours present such a risk to self and/or others that they require detention and care within a secure facility. This legislation establishes a statutory officer called the Director of Forensic Disability to regulate and provide oversight of a newly built medium secure facility for the detention and care of individuals (Forensic Disability Act, 2011). The Director of Forensic Disability reports directly to the Queensland Minister for Communities, Child Safety and Disability Services, but is independent of the Minister when carrying out the functions of that Office. As a further protection in the detention and care of individuals, only the Queensland Mental Health Court (part of the Supreme Court) can make a forensic disability order authorising a person's detention.

The *Positive Futures* programme is a significant reform agenda in Queensland disability services, not only in terms of funding investment in capital works and in increasing specialist staffing but also in terms of the enactment of legislative safeguards around the use of restrictive practices and the establishment of a centre of excellence to drive evidence-based research and practice in positive behaviour support. The Centre of Excellence in Behaviour Support, University of Queensland not only provides training and development to the disability services sector, the centre is instrumental in leading positive behaviour support in Queensland and provides the research evidence to government policies and initiatives. It is important to note that at the time of writing this chapter, there has been a review of the Queensland legislation and changes made to the role of the Centre of Excellence in Behaviour Support.

More recently, Tasmania amended its disability services legislation to give greater emphasis to human rights in line with the CRPD (United Nations, 2006). Similar to Victoria, Tasmania legislated to create the role of the Senior Practitioner to monitor and evaluate the use of restrictive practices. Under the Tasmanian legislation, the powers of the Senior Practitioner are not as extensive as those of the Victorian Senior Practitioner. Interestingly, the Tasmanian legislation also defines restrictive practices differently from Queensland and Victoria. Two types of restrictive practices are defined. First, *environmental restriction*, which is defined as a restrictive intervention in relation to the person that consists of the modification of an object, or the environment of the person, so as to enable the behavioural control of the person but does not include a personal restriction. Secondly, *personal restriction*, which is defined as a restrictive intervention in relation to the person that consists wholly or partially of (a) physical contact with the person so as to enable the behavioural control of the person; or (b) the taking of an action that restricts the liberty of movement of the person (Disability Services Act, 2011). Approval for restrictive practices is governed by the Tasmanian Guardianship and Administration Board which is an independent statutory authority.

As is evident above, there is a significant effort and investment in Australia, at least in some jurisdictions, to protect the rights of people with a disability who are at risk of restrictive practices. These developments are, however, relatively recent, and their impact on the lives of people with a disability subject to restrictive practices will require monitoring and evaluation over a period of time. However, as Victoria was the first Australian state to enact such laws, in 2006, the next section will explore how the strategies implemented in that jurisdiction provide important insights and lessons for future initiatives in this field.

Learning from the Victorian model of protecting rights

Victoria is the second most populous state in Australia, with a population of approximately 5.3 million people (Australian Bureau of Statistics, 2008). Approximately 24,000 Victorians have some form of intellectual disability (learning disability) or cognitive impairment and receive disability funded services from the Victorian Government. In 2006, the Disability Act (2006) established the role of the Senior Practitioner in Victoria to monitor and protect the rights of people with a disability who were subjected to restraint and seclusion in government funded disability services. The Senior Practitioner's main functions are to independently monitor, research, and educate around the use of restrictive interventions and compulsory treatment in disability funded services in Victoria. Analysis regarding this role in terms of good practice is further examined in Chapter 5 of this book.

The establishment of the Senior Practitioner provides a unique opportunity to examine the impact of restraint reduction strategies because all disability service providers in Victoria providing government funded services are required by law to report any chemical restraint (defined as medication for sole purpose of changing behaviour, not used as treatment for an underlying health issue), mechanical restraint (any materials used to prevent movement, except materials used therapeutically or for safe travel) and seclusion (sole confinement) that occurs within their organisation. As of 1 July 2012, disability service providers were also required to report any physical restraint (any use of physical force that is not guidance or assistance).

The Senior Practitioner developed four main strategies to prevent and/or reduce the use of restraint and seclusion.

1. **Leadership for organisational change**

    a. The Senior Practitioner communicated a vision to all disability services about promoting the dignity and rights of all people with a disability and safely reducing the use of restraint and seclusion.

    b. Working with regional leadership groups to find alternatives for people who have complex needs.

    c. Working with professional organisations such as the Australian Psychological Society, the Australasian Society for Intellectual Disability and Disability Professionals Victoria to develop education, practice standards and guidance for their members.

2. **The use of data to inform practice and policy**

    Data is collected on a monthly basis and analysed regarding:

    a. who is subjected to restraint and seclusion (eg age, gender, disability)

    b. where the restraint and seclusion took place, time of the shift, staff involved, and the behaviour of concern that led to the use of restraint or seclusion

    c. effectiveness of restrictive interventions (ratings from service providers)

The findings from the data collected by the Senior Practitioner is shared in all meetings with disability staff and is used to inform the skills and knowledge needed to be included in workforce development. The findings drawn from the data also inform programme development and funding of specific projects, such as: a clinical outreach intervention programme for children and young persons with autism (Senior Practitioner report 2009-10, 2011); the development of training, peer support and a resource kit for speech pathologists working with persons subject to restrictive practices who have complex communication needs; and a chemical restraint reduction strategy, and a roadmap towards prevention of restrictive practices for disability organisations (see Senior Practitioner report 2010-11, 2012).

3. **Workforce development**

   Workforce development has focused on:

   a. understanding individual support needs

   b. how to complete functional behaviour assessments

   c. how to develop focused positive support strategies including de-escalation approaches

   d. how to improve the overall quality of behaviour support planning (Webber, McVilly, Fester and Chan, 2011; Webber, Richardson, Lambrick and Fester, 2012)

   e. development and delivery of human rights training for staff (Office of the Senior Practitioner: Enlivening Human Dignity and Rights, 2009), and

   f. development of a CRPD guide as self-check audit

   g. human rights training for people with a disability and self advocates

4. **Use of restraint and seclusion reduction tools**

   a. Clinical review by specialists to provide suggestions for alternative preventative measures.

   b. Funding for small change projects to encourage disability service providers to find alternatives to restraint and seclusion (Webber, Mountford, Wilson, Andrews and Sturt, 2009).

   c. A series of plain English reviews about alternatives to the use of restrictive interventions such as mindfulness, use of comfort rooms, occupational therapy techniques.

The above strategies are similar to four of the six core strategies found by Azeem, Aujla, Rammerth, Binsfeld and Jones (2011) and Le Bel, Huckshorn and Caldwell (2010) to be important to restraint reduction in mental health. Two other strategies that have not been used in Victoria, but are included in the work in the USA are improving consumer's role in inpatient setting, and vigorous debriefing techniques. Recently, Azeem et al, (2011) examined the impact of these six strategies and reported significant reductions in the use of 'manual' (referred to as physical restraint in UK and Australia) and 'mechanical' restraint and seclusion within a year.

Over the first four years of implementation, these strategies have had a modest, but nevertheless real, impact on the use of restrictive practices in disability services in Victoria. On average, there has been a 2% decrease each year in the total number of people subjected to restraint and seclusion (down 8% over four years). One of the reasons for this modest impact is that the majority of people (96%) subject to restrictive practices during this period were reported to be administered chemical restraint on a routine basis which is prescribed by medical practitioners. Service providers do not have any ability to regulate the use of routine chemical restraint, but they do have control over the use of PRN (as needed) chemical restraint, mechanical restraint and seclusion. Decreases were observed in the use of PRN chemical restraint and in the use of seclusion over the three years. On the other hand, no changes were observed in the use of mechanical restraint. The findings regarding the lack of mechanical restraint reduction is consistent with the literature in that mechanical restraint is one of the more difficult restraints to reduce fowr several reasons, including the finding that people who have been mechanically restrained may engage in self-restraint (Powers, Roane and Kelley, 2007; Rooker and Roscoe, 2005).

These particular findings regarding mechanical restraint are not consistent with the findings by Azeem et al (2011) but it should be noted that Azeem et al (2011) examined physical and mechanical restraint together, so it is not possible to directly compare with the findings of this study. More recently, significant reductions in restraint and seclusion have been found for people whose behaviour support plans achieved a certain level of quality. This was the case for PRN chemical, mechanical restraint and seclusion. This finding suggests that another critical restraint and seclusion reduction strategy is improvement in the quality of support available to people with a disability at risk of restraint and seclusion.

Taken together the findings suggest that the strategies currently in place are not sufficient to reduce the use of all types of restraint and seclusion currently monitored in Victoria. When compared to other work by LeBel et al (2010), Azeem et al (2011) and Sanders (2009), two strategies that are missing to some degree are leadership at an organisational level and debriefing techniques. There is considerable evidence within the broader organisational change research to show that transformational change can only be achieved within organisations when there is a critical mass of people forming a leadership coalition within an organisation (Kotter, 2011). In Victoria, the leadership coalition (headed by the Senior Practitioner) is likely to be too far removed to have an impact on day to day operations. According to Sanders (2009) this leadership coalition must be at the level of the service provider.

Although less is known about the impact of debriefing techniques on the change process in preventing the use of restrictive practices, it is likely that debriefing is a critical strategy in moving away from restrictive interventions towards non-traumatising forms of support. For example, the formal debriefing used by Azeem et al (2011) required staff to examine the incident in a root cause analysis fashion, so that staff had to adopt a rigorous problem-solving procedure to identify what went wrong, what could have been done differently, and how to avoid similar incidents in the future. In addition the debriefing procedure used by Azeem et al (2011) also meant that the interventions needed to mitigate the impact of traumatisation and re-traumatisation to the patient and staff were more likely to be implemented.

It is important to note that the Senior Practitioner in Victoria is predominantly a legislative oversight and monitoring role, and that the legislation is in its seventh year. Chan (2010) argues that while legislative compliance is a critical factor as an overarching legal framework to protect rights through monitoring and regulation, a state-wide practice change strategy at the organisational level is equally important. As such, further consideration ought to be given to how legislation can be reframed to have effect at the organisational levels of leadership, culture and practice. These may include creative incentives for service providers to prevent and reduce the use of restrictive practice (such as reducing insurance premium costs for every reduction or safe elimination of restrictive practice), engaging more broadly key professional bodies and their role in reducing restrictive practices, and investing in practice innovation and workforce development in order to give effect to a paradigm shift from a reliance on restrictive practice use to one of finding creative alternatives as evident in the emerging literature (Chan, 2010; Chan et al, 2012).

In summary, in common with trends in the UK, it could be argued that the strategies used by the Senior Practitioner have to date been effective on a few rather than the many (Whitehead, Curtice, Beyer, McConkey, and Bogues, 2008).

It appears that success in the prevention of restrictive practices depends both on the strategies used to reduce restraint and seclusion and the types of restraints and seclusion to be reduced. At this stage, it remains unknown as to whether the six core strategies specified by LeBel et al (2010) would be effective for reducing all types of restraint and seclusion used in disability services.

Conclusion

This chapter has highlighted the growing movement in Australia to protect the rights of people with intellectual disability and autism who are subject to restrictive practices and compulsory treatment (such as detention and care of forensic disability clients). The legislative frameworks governing restrictive practices in three Australian jurisdictions, and broader contexts for these initiatives have been briefly surveyed, noting some similarities and differences. In each jurisdiction, restrictive practices are constrained by the principle of least restriction and may only be used as a last resort when there is a risk of significant harm to self and/or others. The impact of these legislations is yet to be assessed.

Victoria was the first Australian state to enact laws in relation to the use of restrictive practices to protect the rights of people with disability. Despite the implementation of a number of strategic initiatives in that jurisdiction over the past seven years, only modest gains have been attained in the reduction of certain restrictive practices. Nevertheless these gains are real and substantial for those individuals who are no longer subject to restrictive practices and who are subject to less restriction than previously. It remains to be seen if these gains will be cumulative and sustainable over time.

It has not been within the scope of this chapter to provide in-depth analysis as to whether recent Australian legislative developments have been effective in preventing, reducing, or eliminating restrictive practices. In many ways, it is too early to tell. However it is important to reiterate that legislation does play a critical role in giving effect to rights protection. This is particularly so in Victoria where extensive functions and powers are provided to the Senior Practitioner enabling intervention at the individual and systemic levels and where there is a mandatory requirement on service providers to report on each episode of restrictive practice. Nevertheless, while legislative compliance is important and necessary, it is clear that it is not a sufficient response to the problem of restrictive practices by itself. Chan (2010) argues that a practice change strategy within an organisation is equally important. Cross-sectoral and organisational strategies capable of impacting on organisational leadership, culture and practice at all levels are also required. In particular, leadership at the local level is essential to drive practice and cultural change from one of resorting to restrictive practice use in the first instance to one where human rights become the beacon leading practice development in disability services, and legislation is the leverage in which leadership can draw upon to enforce the safeguarding of rights of people subject to restrictive practices.

References

Australian Bureau of Statistics (2008) Australian Demographic Statistics, Dec 2008, data cube: SuperTABLE, Cat. no. 3235.0.55.001, http://bit.ly/Y4kfzQ [Accessed 1.7.14]

Azeem, M W, Aujla, A, Rammerth, M, Binsfeld, G and Jones R B (2011) Effectiveness of six core strategies based on trauma informed care in reducing seclusions and restraints at a child and adolescent psychiatric hospital. *Journal of Child and Adolescent Psychiatric Nursing*, 24, 11–15

Carter, W J (2006) *Challenging Behaviour and Disability: A targeted response*. Report to the Honourable Warren Pitt, Minister for Communities, Disability Services and Seniors

Chan, J (2010) People with disability subject to restrictive interventions and compulsory treatment: applying human rights to improve disability client outcomes and practice change. In: Naylor, B, Debeljak, J, Dussuyer, I and Thomas, S (eds) *Proceedings of a Roundtable on Monitoring and Oversight of Human Rights in Closed Environments, 29 November 2010, Monash University Law Chambers* (pp. 21–29). Melbourne: Monash University

Chan, J, French, P and Webber, L (2011) Positive behavioural support and the UNCRPD. *International Journal of Positive Behavioural Support*, 1(1), 7–13

Chan, J, French, P, Hudson, C and Webber, L (2011) Applying the CRPD to safeguard the rights of people with a disability in contact with the criminal justice system. *Psychiatry, Psychology and Law*, 19(4), 558–565

Chan, J, LeBel, J and Webber, L (2012) The dollars and sense of restraints and seclusion. *Journal of Law and Medicine*, 20, 73–81

Department of Communities, Child Safety and Disability Services (2013) Review of restrictive practices. Download from: http://bit.ly/1sSkolo [Accessed 1.7.14]

Dimopoulos, A (2010) *Issues in Human Rights Protection of Intellectually Disabled Persons*. Surrey: Ashgate Publishing Limited

Disability Act (2006) Number 23/2006. Victoria, Australia

Disability Services Act (2011) Number 27 of 2011. Tasmania, Australia

Disability Services and Other Legislation Amendment Act (2008) Act No. 23 of 2008. Queensland, Australia

Forensic Disability Act (2011). Queensland, Australia

French, P, Chan, J and Carracher, R (2010) Realising human rights in clinical practice and service delivery to persons with a cognitive impairment who engage in behaviours of concern. *Psychiatry, Psychology and Law*, 17(2), 245–272

Keski-Valkama, A, Sailas, E, Eronen, M, Koivisto, A-M, Lonnqvist, J and Kaltiala-Heino, R (2007) A 15-year national follow-up: legislation is not enough to reduce the use of seclusion and restraint. *Soc Psychiatry Psychiatr Epidemiol*, 42, 747–752

Kotter, J P (2011) Leading change: Why transformation efforts fail. In: *HBR's 10 Must Reads: the essentials* (137-152). Boston, Mass: Harvard Business Review Press

LeBel, J, Huckshorn, KA and Caldwell, B (2010) Restraint use in residential programs: why are best practices ignored? *Child Welfare*, 89(2), 169–187

Northern Territory Bills (2011) *Disability Services Amendment Bill 2012. Serial No. 196*. Darwin, Northern Territory: Legislative Assembly, Northern Territory of Australia

Office of the Senior Practitioner: Enlivening Human Dignity and Rights (2009) *The Senior Practitioner Implementing the Victorian Charter for Human Rights and Responsibilities, 2006: Guidelines for disability service providers and practitioners*. Melbourne, Victoria: Department of Human Services

Office of the Senior Practitioner (2008) *Senior Practitioner Annual Report 2007-2008*. Melbourne, Victoria: Department of Human Services

Office of the Senior Practitioner (2009) *Senior Practitioner Annual Report 2008-2009*. Melbourne, Victoria: Department of Human Services

Office of the Senior Practitioner (2011) *Senior Practitioner Report 2009-10*. Melbourne, Victoria: Department of Human Services

Office of the Senior Practitioner (2012) *Senior Practitioner Report 2010-11*. Melbourne, Victoria: Department of Human Services

Owens, F, Griffiths, D, Tarulli, D and Murphy, J (2009) Historical and theoretical foundations of the rights of persons with intellectual disabilities: setting the stage. In: Owen, F and Griffiths, D (eds) *Challenges to the Human Rights of People with Intellectual Disabilities*. London: Jessica Kingsley Publishers

Positive Futures (2011) *Positive Futures Overview*. Download from: http://bit.ly/1vHkNuE [Accessed 1.7.14]

Powers, K V, Roane, H S and Kelley, M (2007) Treatment of self-restraint associated with the application of protective equipment. *Journal of Applied Behavior Analysis*, 40, 577–581

Ramcharan, B G (2008) *Contemporary Human Rights Ideas*. Oxford: Taylor and Francis

Romijn, A and Frederiks, B J M (2012) Restriction on restraints in the care for people with intellectual disabilities in the Netherlands: lessons learned from Australia, UK, and United States. *Journal of Policy and Practice in Intellectual Disabilities*, 9(2), 127–133

Rooker, G W and Roscoe, E M (2005) Functional analysis of self-injurious behaviour and its relation to self-restraint. *Journal of Applied Behavior Analysis*, 38, 537–542

Sanders, K (2009) The effects of an action plan, staff training, management support and monitoring on restraint use and costs of work-related injuries. *Journal of Applied Research in Intellectual Disabilities*, 22, 216–220

South Australian Social Inclusion Board (2011) *Strong Voices. A Blueprint to Enhance Life and Claim the Rights of People with Disability in South Australia (2012-2020)*. Adelaide, South Australia: Department of the Premier and Cabinet

Sturmey, P (2009) It is time to reduce and safely eliminate restrictive behavioural practices (editorial). *Journal of Applied Research in Intellectual Disabilities*, 22, 105–110

Tsiouris, J A (2010) Pharmacotherapy for aggressive behaviours in persons with intellectual disabilities: treatment or mistreatment? *Journal of Intellectual Disability Research*, 54, 1–16

Tyrer, P, Oliver-Africano, P C, Ahmed, Z, Bouras, N, Cooray, S, Deb, S et al (2006) Risperidone, haloperidol, and placebo in the treatment of aggressive challenging behaviour in patients with intellectual disability: a randomised controlled trial. *The Lancet*, 371, 57–63

United Nations (2006) *Convention on the Rights of Persons with Disabilities and Optional Protocol*. New York, NY: United Nations

United Nations (2008) *Torture and Other Cruel, Inhuman or Degrading Treatment or Punishment: Note by the Secretary-General*, UN GAOR, 63rd Sess., Provisional Agenda Item 67(a), 69, UN Doc A/63/175 (July 28, 2008)

Victorian Law Reform Commission (2003) *People with Intellectual Disabilities at Risk: Report*. Melbourne, Victoria: Victorian Law Reform Commission

Ward, T and Stewart, C (2008) Putting
human rights into practice with people with
an intellectual disability. *J Dev Phys Disabil*,
20:297–311

Webber, L, Lambrick, F, Donley, M,
Buchholtz, M, Chan, J, Carracher, R and
Patel, G (2010) Restraint and seclusion of
people on compulsory treatment orders in
Victoria, Australia in 2008-2009. *Psychiatry,
Psychology and Law*, 17(4), 562–573

Webber, L S, McVilly, K and Chan, J (2011)
Restrictive interventions for people
with a disability exhibiting challenging
behaviours: analysis of a population
database. *Journal of Applied Research in
Intellectual Disabilities*, 24(6), 495–507

Webber, L, McVilly, K, Fester, T and Chan,
J (2011) Factors influencing the quality of
behaviour support plans and the impact
of quality of BSPs on the use of restrictive
interventions in disability services in
Australia. *International Journal of Positive
Behavioural Support*, 1(1), 24–31

Webber, L S, Mountford, L, Wilson, J,
Andrews, B and Sturt, D (2009) *Bright Ideas
for Reducing Restraint*. Australasian Society
for the Study of Intellectual Disability 9th
Annual Conference for Disability Support
Workers, Melbourne

Webber, L S, Richardson, B, Lambrick, F and
Fester, T (2012) The impact of the quality
of behaviour support plans on the use of
restraint and seclusion in disability services.
*International Journal of Positive Behavioural
Support*, 2(2), pp. 3–11

Whitehead, S, Curtice, L, Beyer, S, McConkey,
R and Bogues S (2008) Learning disability
policy in the UK. *Tizard Learning Disability
Review*, 13 (3), 4–11

Chapter 3

Ethical principles and good practice in reducing restrictive practices

Sharon Paley

Introduction

The French psychiatrist, Parchappe, who visited England in 1847, reported on an innovation at Gloucester Asylum, which at that time was under the direction of Samuel Hitch, the forward thinking psychiatrist and founder of the first psychiatric association in 1841.

Parchappe commented:

> "This is quite an exceptional arrangement. The patients who work in the gardens occupy special quarters consisting of a kitchen-refectory with an open fire and a dormitory with 14 beds. The patients live here by themselves; the door is open directly to the gardens and is outside the asylum wall. They are supervised only by the head gardener who lives in a cottage at some distance. They go to bed at 8, get up when they like. They come and go freely just as they wish. If they wish to go into the town they have only to ask the gardener's permission. The establishment provides them with meat, bread and beer, and the gardener gives them fruit and vegetables; they do their own cooking and run their household for themselves. The medical superintendent claims that no inconvenience of any kind has resulted from this peculiar arrangement, and this seems to show how very far one can go in introducing into institutions conditions as nearly as possible resembling those of ordinary life."

This report was particularly remarkable at that time given that most asylums operated within the confines of high walls and locked gates; people were not free to leave at will nor were they afforded any control over their day to day life in terms of what they would eat, when they would get up or how they would run the 'household'. Many people were effectively secluded and some may have been restrained. At that time people who were regarded as 'insane' would have included those who would now be regarded as having an intellectual disability.

From the above short extract it is clear that the idea of an 'ordinary life', as set out in John O'Brien's five service accomplishments, (O'Brien, 1987) being appropriate for people otherwise segregated from society, is not as new as perhaps we would like to believe. In 1847 it was clear that the benefits of freedom and liberty to people experiencing a psychiatric illness, or having an intellectual disability, were understood by the leading practitioners of the time.

What is restriction, deprivation or containment?

When discussing restrictive practices within the field of social care and health it is possible to define a number of practices as restrictive practices. Broadly speaking, restrictive practices definitions include:

- **Physical intervention or physical restraint** is the application of force by one person or more, towards another in order to restrict their freedom of movement.

- **Mechanical restraint** is the application of belts, straps or aids, which will prevent the free mobilisation of the person or their limbs at will.

- **Chemical restraint** is the use of drugs in order to control the behaviour of a person when there is no other therapeutic benefit in the prescribing of the medication.

- **Psychological restraint** is using rules or threats, real or imaginary, in order to prevent a person acting freely and at will (this may on occasions be discussed or described as social restraint).

- **Environmental restraint** is changing the environment of a person or placing them in an environment which restricts their freedom of movement and effectively prevents them leaving that space or area.

- **A restriction** is the act of limiting or controlling an individual (possibly by regulation or law) in a way that will reduce their freedom.

- **A deprivation** is to lose and be disadvantaged by the removal of personal freedoms which may be yours as a right (a deprivation may be applied by regulation).

- **Containment** is the act of keeping 'something' or someone under control by using external mechanisms, rules or force.

Restrictive practices remain contentious in the field of intellectual disability as well as in wider human services. Some practitioners (Cambridge, 2002, McDonnell, 2009) have gone as far as suggesting that legislation and policy discussing the appropriate use of restrictive practices in some way authorises their application and use. It has been suggested that euphemisms are used by society in order to decriminalise crimes committed against people with intellectual disability. For example, a restraint used in a service may in other contexts be viewed as 'assault' and seclusion would be seen as 'false imprisonment'. In the face of such contentious arguments the use and application of restrictive practices within human services presents challenges to professionals and others which require careful consideration. This chapter will explore ethical decision making in relation to the reduction in restrictive practices, with reference to a UK setting. It will then explore two models for ethical decision making that could guide family members and paid workers in their decision making when supporting a person who challenges to have a good quality of life.

Ethical and human rights principles

Ethics can be defined as a set of principles and values by which an individual, a group or organisation operate. Morals are founded on the fundamental principles of our ethical beliefs. Ethics is about deciding on a particular course of action, and ethical decision making is about enabling people to decide what is the right way to act in particular circumstances (Giarchi, 2012). It is often the case that an individual's professional and ethical framework is underpinned by their beliefs and it is the two factors combined which underpin their actions. Giarchi (2012) explains that the ethics of health and social care operate within a complex set of normative 'pulls' that can at times be in tension. The 'pulls' that professionals might consider in relation to a particular ethical decision include:

- the individual's moral framework

- the values of those involved, for example those of the person receiving support, their family members and paid workers

- the wider policy and legal context

- the professional's codes of conduct, when this is relevant

Ethical dilemmas are faced daily by those working in health and social care and who support people with intellectual disabilities whose behaviour challenges services. This can include balancing the potential benefits and risks of taking a particular course of action. For example, a team may need to decide whether or not it is in someone's best interest to be subject to a physical restraint to reduce episodes of self harming. Some team members may be opposed to such a course of action, whilst others may believe that the best interests of the client outweigh any ethical concerns related to such an intervention being applied.

The individual's moral framework

Individuals have a personal set of beliefs and values which affect how they behave and the way in which they work. Their core beliefs and values will have been influenced by personal experiences including family circumstances, cultural experience, religious beliefs and wider life experience. At work these personal values can be influenced, and modified, by the principles and values of the organisation employing them. For example, for people working in an NHS organisation in England these will be informed by the NHS Constitution (Department of Health, 2013). Members of staff would be expected to use the values and principles of their employer to inform the decisions they make and the support they provide, even if these were potentially at odds with their own personal values.

The values of those involved, including the person receiving support, their family members and paid workers

Recent legislation and models of support have promoted the empowerment of people with an intellectual disability so that they can have a greater say in the support they receive as well as opportunities to influence services. There has been an increased emphasis on providing independent advocacy, involving people and family members and empowering them in their support and care (Department of Health 2009a, Department of Health, Social Services and Public Safety 2011, Duffy 2006).

In considering wider values and approaches, it is helpful to consider models of care and support and how they have evolved to influence services and those who work within them. In the last half century, support for people with an intellectual disability has been influenced by a number of leading thinkers and practitioners including John O'Brien (1987), Wolf Wolfensberger (1972, 1980) and Jim Mansell (et al) (2010, 2007, 2001). Some of their work, values and ideas have influenced broader social and health care policies as well as those specifically relating to support for people with an intellectual disability. Their work and that of others has influenced the national agenda and in turn that of organisational policy, direction and mission, which provides an impact on the way in which individuals support people.

The wider policy and legal context

It is important that legislation, policy and guidance is understood and used to inform ethical decision making. This might include human rights legislation, capacity and safeguarding legislation, policies relating to health and social care as well as national strategies such as Valuing People Now (Department of Health, 2009a), Protecting Patients from Avoidable Harm (Department of Health, 2013) and the NHS Constitution (Department of Health, 2013).

There is good evidence that human rights legislation is having an increasing impact on the wider legislative and policy context related to the support of people with intellectual disabilities. This is particularly true when considering issues related to the use of restrictive practices. For example, the Human Rights Act 1998 and the United Nations Convention on the Rights of Person with Disabilities 2006 have relevance specific to the use of restrictive practices.

The professional's codes of conduct, when this is relevant

Most health and social care professions have their own code of conduct or code of practice; these are made up of moral principles that form the basis of professional standards or rules covering a wide range of subjects from confidentiality to reporting abuse (Banks, 2006, Cuthbert and Qualington 2008). This ensures that professional standards are informed by the legal framework. Professional standards are often supported by a complaints and compliance system that can apply sanctions to professionals for serious breaches. In the UK, codes of conduct relating to professional workers such as nurses, doctors and social workers have been established by the national Nursing and Midwifery

Council, the General Medical Council, the British Medical Association and the Health Professions Council.

The four 'virtuous obligations' of medical ethics developed by Beauchamp and Childress (2008) are often used to underpin professional codes of conduct and ethical decision making. These can also be applied to decision making in relation to restraint reduction. However, practitioners need to consider how these might concur or conflict with the individual's own values and how they might be culturally and time specific. Beauchamp and Childress's (2008) four virtuous obligations are:

- **Beneficence** – do what is good, provide benefits to persons and contribute to their welfare. Actions that are taken in the best interest of the person.

- **Non-maleficence** – avoid causing harm. The obligation not to inflict harm intentionally or through an act of omission.

- **Respect for autonomy** – respecting the person's entitlement to make their own decisions. Acknowledge a person's right to make choices, to hold views, and to take actions based on personal values and beliefs.

- **Justice** – To treat others equitably, adhere to the rights, social and cultural norms of society, ensure a fair distribution of benefits and risks.

The virtuous obligations are often useful in understanding and articulating the issues to be considered when faced with a complex decision. However, they do not directly assist with the actual decision making process.

When giving consideration to the above four obligations, it is clear how these can be applied to services for people who have an intellectual disability. They are consistent with person centred values; they reinforce the autonomy of the person and the best interests of the individual are reflected in the beneficence obligations when applied to human services.

The United Nations' *Convention on the Rights of Persons with Disabilities* in the context of restrictive practices and ethics

Relevant literature over a number of years suggests that people who have an intellectual disability and who also exhibit challenging behaviour are commonly exposed to aversive practices including restrictive interventions, such as physical restraint or chemical restraint (Baker and Allen, 2001, Allen, 2008, Deb, 2009, Chan et al, 2013).The efficacy of such restrictive practices is poor, in terms of restrictive practices being effective at eliminating the identified challenging behaviour. The therapeutic benefits of restrictive practices are a cause for concern when one considers the international literature. Much of the available research concludes that there is little therapeutic value in the use of restrictive practices, and in fact there are particular risks associated with their use and application (Paterson et al, 2003, Paterson, 2003, Paley, 2006, McVilley, 2008, Leadbetter and Paterson, 2009, Nunno, 2011).

Leadbetter (2009) explained that the term 'therapeutic' implies that positive change will occur as the consequence of the identified intervention being applied. However, he considers that this is not the case with most restrictive practices. Furthermore Chan et al (2013) have suggested that *"recently, there has been an emergence of the application of a human rights paradigm to clinical practice and service delivery to people with learning disability and challenging behaviours"*. International legislation and guidance is drawing upon human rights principles when discussing restrictive practices and the support of people with intellectual disability (Australasian Psychological Society, 2011, Ministry of Justice, 2008, Carter, 2006). Increasingly, the research is making a direct link between the efficacy and evidence of restrictive practices and human rights principles being applied to the support of people who have intellectual disability and challenging behaviour.

It is helpful to consider these issues in the context of the United Nations' Convention on the Rights of Persons with Disabilities (CRPD) (2006). The CRPD is an internationally accepted convention that states that individuals should be 'guaranteed freedom from torture and from cruel, inhumane or degrading treatment or punishment' (Article 15). In addition, it states that countries should 'protect the physical and mental integrity of persons with disabilities, just as for everyone else' (Article 17) and 'enact laws and administrative measures to guarantee freedom from exploitation, violence and abuse' (Article 16). In considering the use and application of restrictive practices it is possible to argue that they could:

- be cruel, inhumane or degrading towards a person exposed to them

- possibly cause physical and mental harm to a person through physical injury or psychological trauma

- be experienced by a person who is exposed to their use as violent, abusive or coercive practices

It can be helpful for practitioners to use frameworks which account for the CRPD when giving consideration to the ethical aspect of any intervention, including a planned restrictive practice. Having consideration for such principles will help to determine whether a specific approach is both appropriate in the context of an individual's assessed need and the least restrictive intervention possible in the circumstances. As such:

- People should not be exposed to 'therapies' or 'treatments' which are degrading or demeaning to that person; this would include controversial therapies or interventions for which the evidence base is poor or lacking.

- People should not be exposed to bullying, intimidation or practices which rely on aversive outcomes to gain control over the person. Historically, reducing behaviours often described as challenging might include aversive approaches such as squeezing lemon juice into someone's mouth when they do a behaviour that others want to change. However, some more 'acceptable' approaches, including the removal of perceived 'privileges' (such as a trip out or a fish and chip supper) from people also rely on an aversive outcome.

- People should not be denied access to basic supports – individuals and organisations should not prevent people from having access to day to day necessities such as food, water, meaningful occupation or required healthcare. People with intellectual disabilities have difficulties in accessing basic rights such as the right to work; only 10% of people who have an intellectual disability who receive a service in the UK are known to be in paid employment (Department of Health, 2009b) which in itself can contribute to social isolation and behaviours that are challenging.

- People should not be denied the opportunity and support to use their preferred means of communication so that they can be heard as an autonomous being; how often do we hear comments like 'oh, he understands everything you say', yet what you observe does not even come close to replicating the usual exchange of communication experienced by other people? How do we know that he 'understands everything you say' and if this is the case why is that person receiving instruction and not engaging in his support?

- People should not be imprisoned or otherwise restricted without lawful excuse. On occasions, there are well intended restrictions occurring as a result of a 'perceived' risk to people. These can include locks on doors to prevent access to a kitchen, garden or front path because staff teams worry about a perceived risk, and not an actual risk. No one can be restricted without lawful excuse and any act of restriction must be reasonable and proportionate to the risk which is being managed.

- People should not be exposed to assault or abuse, or act in any way that causes physical pain or serious psychological distress; or involve the unauthorised use of medication. Sadly, there are instances of people who have an intellectual disability and children being abused throughout history (eg Department of Health and Social Security, 1969, BBC, 1999, Healthcare Commission, 2007, Flynn, 2012, Estyn, 2012).

- People should not be exposed to any practice that places limits on personal freedom, choice and expressions without lawful excuse. Recently the 'blue room' case in England demonstrated how a practice which might appear to be therapeutic and helpful to the individual is in reality an abusive and unlawful approach, (R (C) v A Local Authority and Others [2011] EWHC 1539 (Admin)).

Adapted from Australasian Psychological Society, 2011

There is a long history of people's rights being disregarded in very obvious ways in human services; it is a sad fact that many of the high profile abuse cases involving vulnerable people have highlighted the abusive use of restrictive practices (BBC, 1999, BBC, 2011, Flynn, 2012). The abuse of vulnerable people by those who are charged with a duty to provide them support and care is a breach of trust and a breach of the human rights of the individual with a disability. Most recently in the UK there was the Winterbourne View Hospital scandal, associated with the televising of the terrible abuse of a number of people with intellectual disabilities broadcast by the BBC Panorama programme in May 2011 (BBC, 2011). Eleven care workers, including qualified registered nurses were charged with and found guilty of offences related to this case. Such abuse is easily recognised as an illegal practice as it is so severe and shocking. It is clear when viewing the footage that the intention of the perpetrators is to cause harm, distress and suffering.

What is trickier is deciding when a practice or therapy may be legitimate and in a person's best interest, but includes aspects that may also infringe that person's rights. There can be many ethical, moral and legal conflicts in such situations. A major challenge for many professionals is actually recognising when a practice, that has good intentions, may be a breach of someone's human rights and the legislative framework. This chapter will go on to explore some of these fundamental issues.

A model for ethical decision making

This model (figure 1) has been specifically developed to address the areas to be considered when an ethical dilemma arises in relation to restraint reduction. In this model, the person is placed at the centre to ensure that they are included in the decision making process as far as possible and that their representatives or advocates are consulted. This person centred approach is firmly in line with the values and principles articulated in recent policies (Mansell 2007, Department of Health 2009a).

To work in an ethically informed way, it is important to adopt a person centred approach that is respectful of the person and their individuality and supports them to achieve their goals in life. The model is primarily person centred and multi-factorial in its approach to ethical decision making. It indicates that a multidisciplinary team should undertake a functional analysis of the behaviour as part of any behavioural assessment. This will enable the multidisciplinary team to understand better the function of the behaviour and to decide on an appropriate intervention plan, to reduce the risk of the behaviour. This approach considers the person in the context of their life experience, family situation and social experiences.

This case study illustrates how this model can be applied to a specific situation.

Steven is a 21 year old man who has autism and severe intellectual disability. He lives with his mother, an older sister who is 23 and younger twin brothers who are 16. Over many years, Steven has exhibited some self-injurious behaviours, but these have been low level hand biting and head slapping which the family have felt able to cope with. Recently Steven spent time on a planned respite holiday. He has family respite with a couple, Mr and Mrs Davies who have no young children

Figure 1   **A model for ethical decision making**

and are semi-retired. While on holiday at the coast, his self-injurious behaviour increased significantly and he started to bite his hand and lower arm, causing small wounds which he picked and subsequently dirt and sand got into the wounds. This behaviour has continued since his return home from holiday and the family are finding it distressing. Steven's Mum is reluctant to take him out in public because his wounds bleed and she feels that other people find his behaviour unacceptable. A discussion has started with the team that support the family as to whether it may be helpful to provide Steven with mittens to stop him being able to pick at his wounds. An alternative would be to have some arm splints made that the family can use to stop him biting himself.

Using the described model of ethical decision making in this situation means:

1. Taking account of the indicators of a behavioural assessment and behavioural risk assessment.

    Ensure that the function of the behaviour has been assessed and that the behavioural interventions are addressing the function of the behaviour. Might the primary and secondary behaviour responses require some adjustment? Can the family apply the recommended behaviour approaches in a consistent way and if not, what can be done to assist?

    How is Steven being occupied and what is he doing at times when he is not exhibiting a self-injurious behaviour?

2. Taking account of the environmental risk assessment.

    What indicators and setting conditions increase the risk of the behaviour occurring? Does the behaviour occur more frequently in certain places or during certain activities? It will be important to evaluate why the behaviour increased when the holiday took place and whether the holiday might in some way have been the trigger for an increase in the behaviour?

    It will also be important to assess the real physical or psychological risk to Steven presented by his self-injuring behaviour. This might have an implication on any decisions reached by the multidisciplinary team related to primary and secondary interventions or restrictive practices.

3. Being based on multidisciplinary decision making protocols.

    Everyone who is involved in supporting Steven and his family should be involved in developing any plan. It will be important that any interventions which are used are applied consistently by everyone and that the views of all involved professionals are sought in this process.

4. Including a review of the evidence base of any agreed approach.

   It will be important to explore the evidence for the application of mechanical restraints in order to manage self-injurious behaviour specific to the population of people who have autism and intellectual disability. What does the published evidence say about the use of mittens or splints? What is the quality of that evidence, single case studies versus peer reviewed articles? Are there multiple studies to support the use of mechanical restraint across the published research and if so what is the context? Could it be applied to this situation?

5. Taking account of personal, cultural and social factors that are important to the individual.

   Steven lives in the family home and is one of four children. How practical or otherwise might such a strategy be? Will the family be able to implement the intervention? What circumstances affect them which may mean the intervention might not be appropriate, for example, time, social validity of the approach or the family's perception of the use of mechanical restraint?

6. Being embedded in sound organisational policy, procedural and guidance frameworks. This should be reflected in individualised plans.

   Steven has respite outside of the family home which is provided by another family one weekend a month. How will the use of a mechanical restraint be supported by the policy from the service that supports the respite family? Does the service have a policy which might prevent the use of a mechanical device? In the event that a device is used, it will be important to ensure that there is organisational policy, practice guidance and training offered to both Steven's family and Mr and Mrs Davies.

7. Being subject to continuous review, audit and reflection.

   Adopting approaches that review progress will be important to evaluate any decisions which are taken with regard to interventions. For example, considering a balanced best interest and risk informed decision as to whether or not a mechanical restraint is used in order to reduce the immediate risk to Steven associated with the behaviour. Ongoing review will also consider how to reduce the use of any restrictive practice through the application of robust positive behaviour support responses.

The ethics of restriction, deprivation and containment in services for people who have an intellectual disability

Discussions on the use of restrictive practices and on good practice in supporting a person who challenges will almost inevitably come back to this ethical issue.

> The restriction of people is an infringement of their human rights; it is an infringement of that person's autonomy and individuality and can only be considered to be harmful as an approach within human services.
>
> V
>
> However, due to the prevailing risks, there are occasions when it is absolutely necessary and in that person's best interest to restrict their freedoms and rights in order to reduce the likelihood of harm to them. Indeed you may have a duty of care to protect them (or others) from harm.

On occasions it is appropriate, proportionate and in a person's best interest that a restriction is applied in a particular situation. The family members or paid workers supporting them may also have a duty of care to the person. People have a right to expect that they are supported well and that the professionals and support staff employed to offer support to others owe them a duty of care. The duty of care extends to anyone who may be affected by the professional's actions, judgements or indeed omissions.

On some occasions it is ethically appropriate to restrict an individual's liberty; for example when that restriction will prevent a greater harm. In the case of *RK v (1) BCC (2) YB (3) AK)* [2011] EWCA Civ 1305, the court found that in exercising parental responsibility an adult may impose, or authorise others to impose, restrictions upon the liberty of a child; but such restrictions may not in their totality amount to a deprivation of liberty. Detention engages Article 5 of the Rights of the Child and a parent may not lawfully detain or authorise the detention of a child. It is clear from this judgement, which related to a request by the parent that the local authority provides care for their daughter under Section 20 of the Children Act (UK), that in some circumstances a proportionate and limited restriction is found to be in the best interest of a child.

When considering the ethics of restriction, deprivation and containment in services for adults who have intellectual disability, it is also important to consider the application of the legislative framework applied to children and young people and what the action or practice is. Recently, in a debate about the use of rooms for seclusion, a professional explained that they had developed an approach for managing the behaviour of a young man with severe intellectual disability and autism. It was explained that when the man (who was said to be 19) became aggressive he was 'placed in a tent' (this was inside the house in which he lived) until he is calm, and then he is 'let out.' The professional argued that this was not a restriction of the person's liberty as it was a controlled approach which they had, as a professional, 'signed off' with other people, including the young man's parents and it was part of a 'time out strategy'.

It may be helpful to apply Beauchamp and Childress's (2008) four virtuous obligations, *beneficence, non-maleficence, respect for autonomy and justice*, in considering this specific situation further.

Is the young man choosing to go into the tent?

> *No because it is clear he is placed in the tent by other people; when considering this action in the context of Beauchamp and Childress's (2008) four virtuous obligations it is clear that the young man is not making his own decision to go into the tent. The decision is not an autonomous one.*

Does the young man have any control over this action?

> *Probably not considering the account of the practice and possibly the impact of his learning disability.*

Is this strategy likely to reduce the target behaviour of being aggressive to others and if so how?

> *It is unlikely given that it further isolates him from others and (depending on the impact of his disability) he is unlikely to use the time alone for self-reflection. In addition, there is a lack of evidence that seclusion will reduce the risk associated with any behaviour that is challenging. One must question the benefit of the seclusion to the young man. It is also possible to argue that the strategy may cause psychological trauma and lead to long term harm to the young man. Thus being counter to both beneficence and non-maleficence.*

Can he leave the tent of his own free will?

Probably not. If he has a severe learning disability and autism it is probable that he would not be able to operate a zipper so he is effectively restricted by the action. It is easily argued that restricting someone's freedom to the extent that they cannot leave an area of their own volition might constitute an unlawful restriction or deprivation. In considering that, there is evidence that the intervention is counter to the principles of beneficence and non-maleficence. Overall there is good evidence that the intervention is also contravening the principle of justice.

As a strategy is it the least restrictive option?

It is unlikely that it is the least restrictive option given that this is occurring in his own home and 'time out' (if appropriate) might be more usefully undertaken in another area of the home. As it is not the least restrictive option, one can argue that of all the principles of the four virtuous obligations are breached by the intervention described. This will not be in the man's best interest if an alternative and less restrictive practice might afford him the same or better outcome.

Is there an evidence base for this approach?

I am not aware of any evidence that indicates people who have a severe intellectual disability and autism can be effectively supported by strategies which include forced isolation as a response to risky behaviours and this is contrary to the virtuous principles of beneficence and non-maleficence.

Can a group of professionals including parents 'sign off' a practice and make it lawful?

No. In the case of professionals it will make them and the service that employs them corporately responsible and accountable if the practice is found to be unlawful. As he is over 18 the man's parents cannot lawfully authorise a deprivation. His parents may be consulted as to what is in his best interest within the Mental Capacity Act 2005, as the Act is effective from aged 16. This means that legally there is evidence that the principle of justice is being breached.

The professional believed that because they were not using a room to confine the person, the practice was not seclusion; however, they had not given due consideration to the level of deprivation to which they were exposing the young man. It is probable that a court would find such a practice to be an unlawful deprivation of the person's liberty. Ethically, there is no evidence that such an approach is likely to benefit a person, as there is a lack of evidence for this approach and the account is not consistent with the behavioural principles of time out (Paley, 2009).

It is likely that had the model in figure 1 suggested earlier in this chapter been applied to this decision at an early stage the team would have identified:

- that there was no evidence that forced isolation or seclusion of people with intellectual disability is likely to decrease the risk of the behaviour or risk to the person themselves

- that forced isolation may increase risk to the young person

- that the risks associated with forced isolation were probably higher than the risks of the behaviour for which the intervention is being used

- that national policy guidance does not support the use of seclusion outside of the parameters of the Mental Health Act 1983

The use of medication for purposes other than intended is a further example of an area of ethical debate when considering restrictive practices. It has been found that between 20 and 50% of institutionalised people that have an intellectual disability are prescribed psychotropic medication (Deb and Fraser, 2004). This is despite the fact that evidence to support its use, for the management of behaviours that are challenging, is not well established (Deb, 2009). There is an absence of evidence that the prescription of such medications has a place in the contemporary treatment of people who have an intellectual disability (Deb, 2005).

It is possible to formulate an argument that the prescription of medication to 'control behaviour' is questionable as a practice in intellectual disability and lacks efficacy and evidence. To the extent that it is used to 'control' behaviour it can also be considered a restriction to the person prescribed. A further example of the inappropriate use of medication is the use of Androcur (an anti-libidinal medication prescribed to men) to prevent inappropriate socio-sexual behaviour in men with intellectual disabilities. Given the side effects of such medication which includes gynaecomastia, restlessness, depressive mood states and in rare instances liver disorders or even cancer, it should not be considered as a first option when supporting people who perhaps, might more usefully, be supported to understand what behaviour is or is not appropriate. It is not the least restrictive option available and arguably might do more harm than good in the long term.

One of the most contentious areas relating to restrictions remains the use of physical interventions or physical restraint and its use within the field of intellectual disabilities. Paterson and Bradley (2009) undertook a review of restraint related deaths of people with intellectual disabilities and concluded that *"prone restraint is clearly contraindicated in the presence of obesity and other risk factors. It should therefore be prohibited or subject to the most stringent controls."* Any form of restraint is indeed a restrictive practice and poses a considerable level of risk.

In addition the literature suggests that risk is also associated with specific techniques of physical interventions or restraint, (McVilley, 2008, Wooderson, 2010, Paterson, 2003, 2009, Paley, 2006, Paley-Wakefield, 2012). These may include:

- the use of prone restraint, forcibly holding a person face down on the floor or other surface such as bed or chair

- use of supine restraint, forcibly holding a person in the face up position as they lie on a floor or other surface such as a bed

- wraps or basket holds, holding a person in such a manner that their arms are wrapped round their torso or held at their side or wrapping hands or arms around a person's torso in order to restrict movement

- take-down procedures in which people are taken to the floor against their will forwards or backwards

- bending a person forwards so their head and chest are resting on their thighs and any physical technique that has the effect of pushing the person's head forward onto their chest

- any physical restraint that has the purpose or effect of gaining a person's compliance through the infliction of pain, hyper extension or hyper flexion of the joints

- any physical technique which is based on applying pressure to the chest, abdomen or joints

A human rights perspective on reducing restrictive practices in intellectual disability and autism

It is abundantly clear from the evidence that a range of physical intervention techniques can lead to a significant and at times fatal risk for the person exposed to them. In the context of the ethical debate, one has to question whether such interventions should continue to be employed by human services. Legally and ethically the question is how often are staff supporting children, young people and adults with intellectual disabilities exposed to behaviours that present a risk which is potentially fatal; if the answer to that question is rarely, then there can be little argument to justify the use of physical intervention techniques.

This means that services need to adopt approaches that are aimed at reducing and eventually eradicating restrictive practices whilst introducing frameworks that build on human rights principles putting the person in control and central to the decisions which affect them and their support.

Conclusion

Ethical principles and decision making models do not, on their own, provide a solution when considering an ethical dilemma. They are a means to an end. They help to identify the important factual and ethical issues to take into account. In each situation, those involved must analyse and deliberate on each ethical matter and come to a decision, confident in the knowledge that all of the relevant issues have been considered.

In human services it is important that any legal consideration should also be balanced by an ethical decision making process when exploring issues related to any form of restrictive practice. Each intervention must be reasonable and proportionate given the presenting risk and it should be clear that there are quality of life gains for the individual who is central to any strategy or approach. When considering the ethics of any approach, one must be sure that there is an evidence base for the planned action, in terms of its use and application. In addition, it is important that no harm will be caused to the person, consistent with the obligations of beneficence and non-maleficence (Beauchamp and Childress, 2008).

It can sometimes be the case that good intentions lead to poor practice decisions and poor outcomes for the person involved. Sometimes this is out of a desire to solve a problem, or in the misguided belief that no one else could help the individual or that there are no other options. An act of omission is as potentially dangerous as an intended act of harm. Reactive practices that fail to consider all of the facts have the power to undermine the autonomy, rights, choices and independence of the person being supported. Although the majority of family members, paid workers and professionals intend to help the person they are supporting and to do no harm, when weighing up the ethical issues in relation to restrictive practice this is often not enough. Instead, a sound knowledge of the law and how it can be applied to day to day practice, strong person centred values and a framework for ethical decision making can enable a more reflective and considered approach.

References

Allen, D (2008) The relationship between challenging behaviour and mental ill-health, in people with intellectual disabilities. *Journal of Intellectual Disabilities*, 12(4), 267–294

Australasian Psychological Society (2011) *Evidence-Based Guidelines to Reduce the Need for Restrictive Practices in the Disability Sector*. Melbourne., Victoria, Australia

Baker, P and Allen, D (2001) Physical abuse and physical interventions in learning disabilities: an element of risk? *Journal of Adult Protection*, 3(2), 25–31

Banks, S (2006) *Ethics and Values in Social Work* (third edition). Basingstoke: Palgrave Macmillan

BBC (1999) *MacIntyre Undercover*. Broadcast November 1999

BBC (2011) *Undercover Care: The abuse exposed*. BBC Panorama first shown on 31 May 2011

Beauchamp, T L and Childress, J F (2008) *Principles of Biomedical Ethics*. Oxford: Oxford University Press

Bewley, T. *Madness to Mental Illness. A History of the Royal College of Psychiatrists*. Online archive 4, *Samuel Hitch (1800–1881) (founder of the Association of Medical Officers of Asylums and Hospitals for the Insane)*. Download from: http://bit.ly/1vvWBGb [accessed 1 July 2014]

Cambridge, P (2002) The risks of getting it wrong: systems failure and the impact of abuse. In: Allen, D (ed) *Ethical Approaches to Physical Interventions. Volume I: Responding to challenging behaviour in people with intellectual diabilities*. Birmingham: BILD Publications

Carter, W J (2006) *Challenging Behaviour and Disability: A targeted response*. Report to the Honourable Warren Pitt, Minister for Communities, Disability Services and Seniors

Chan, J, French, P and Webber, L (2013) Positive behavioural support and the UNCRPD. *International Journal of Positive Behavioural Support*. 1(1), 7–13

Cuthbert, S and Quallington, J (2008) *Values for Care Practice*. Health and Social Care: Theory and Practice Series. Exeter: Reflect Press Ltd

Deb, S (2005) The use of psychotropic drugs in people with intellectual disabilities (153–162). In: Roy, A, Roy, M and Clarke, D (eds) *The Psychiatry of Intellectual Disability*. Oxon: Radcliffe Publishing

Deb, S (2009) Ethical use of medication to manage imminent disturbed/violent behaviour in adults with intellectual disabilities. In: Allen, D (ed) *Ethical Approaches to Physical Interventions. Volume II: Changing the agenda.* Birmingham: BILD

Deb, S and Fraser, W (2004) The use of psychotropic medication in people with learning disability: towards rational prescribing. *Human Psychopharmacology: Clinical and Experimental*, 9(4), 259–272

Department of Health (2009a) *Valuing People Now: A new three-year strategy for people with learning disabilities.* London: DH

Department of Health (2009b) *Valuing Employment Now – Real Jobs for People with Learning Disabilities.* London: DH

Department of Health (2013) *NHS Constitution.* London: DH

Department of Health (2013) *Protecting Patients from Avoidable Harm.* London: DH

Department of Health and Social Security (1969) *Report of the Committee of Inquiry into Allegations of Ill Treatment of Patients and other Irregularities at the Ely Hospital, Cardiff.* London: HMSO

Department of Health, Social Services and Public Safety (2011) *Learning Disability Service Framework.* Belfast: Department of Health, Social Services and Public Safety

Duffy, S (2006) *The Keys to Citizenship: A guide to getting good support for people with learning disabilities.* Sheffield: The Centre for Welfare Reform

Estyn (2012) *A Survey of the Arrangements for Pupils' Wellbeing and Behaviour Management in Pupil Referral Units.* Cardiff: Estyn

Flynn, M (2012) *Winterbourne View Hospital: A serious case review.* South Gloucestershire Safeguarding Adults Board

Giarchi, G (2012) The ethics triad: virtues, values and codes of practice. In: Katz, E et al, *Adult Lives: A life course perspective.* Bristol: The Policy Press

Healthcare Commission (2007) *Investigation into the Service for People with Learning Disabilities Provided by Sutton and Merton Primary Care Trust.* London: Commission for Healthcare Audit and Inspection

Human Rights Act 1998. Available to download at www.legislation.gov.uk

Leadbetter, D and Paterson, B (2009) Towards restraint free care. In: Hughes, R (ed) *Reducing Restraints in Health and Social Care: Practice and policy perspectives.* Huntington: Quay Books

Levy, A and Kahan, B J (1991) *The Pindown Experience and the Protection of Children: The report of the Staffordshire Child Care Inquiry 1990.* Stafford: Staffordshire County Council

Mansell, J (2007) *Services for People with Learning Disabilities and Challenging Behaviour or Mental Health Needs*. London: DH

Mansell, J (2010) *Raising our Sights: Services for adults with profound intellectual and multiple disabilities*. London: DH

Mansell, J and Beadle-Brown, J (2010) Deinstitutionalisation and community living: position statement of the Comparative Policy and Practice Special Interest Research Group of the International Association for the Scientific Study of Intellectual Disabilities. *Journal of Intellectual Disability Research*, 54(2), 104–112

Mansell, J, McGill, P and Emerson, E (2001) Development and evaluation of innovative residential services for people with severe intellectual disability and serious challenging behaviour. In: Glidden, L M (ed) *International Review of Research in Mental Retardation*, 24, 245–298. New York: Academic Press

McDonnell, A (2009) *Reducing Restrictive Practices. Tip of the Iceberg. Developing Person Centred Specialist Services*. Birmingham: South Birmingham NHS Trust

McVilley, K (2008) *Physical Restraint in Disability Services: Current practices, contemporary concerns and future directions*. A report commissioned by the Office of the Senior Practitioner, Department of Human Services, Victoria

Ministry of Justice (2008) *Mental Capacity Act Deprivation of Liberty Safeguards*. London: TSO

Nunno, M (2011) *Longitudinal Study of Toxic Child Care Facilities*. Presentation at BILD Positive Behaviour Support Conference, Hinckley Island, Leicestershire, 4–6 May, 2011. Birmingham: BILD

O'Brien, J (1987) A guide to lifestyle planning. In: Wilcox, B and Bellamy, T (eds) *A Comprehensive Guide to the Activities Catalog*. Baltimore: Paul Brookes Publishing

Paley, S (2006) Risk in the context of physical interventions. In: Paley, S and Brooke, J (eds) *Good Practice in Physical Interventions*. Birmingham: BILD

Paley, S (2009) Seclusion and time out: questioning and defining practice. In: Allen, D (ed) *Ethical Approaches to Physical Interventions. Volume II: Changing the agenda*. Birmingham: BILD

Paley-Wakefield, S (2012) Is legislation needed to limit the restraint of clients? *Learning Disability Practice*, 15(3), 24

Paterson, B (2003) Restraint related deaths in health and social care in the UK: learning the lessons. *Mental Health Practice*, 6(9), 11–17

Paterson, B and Bradley, P (2009) Restraint-related deaths: lessons for policy and practice from Tragedy? In: Allen D (ed) *Ethical Approaches to Physical Interventions. Volume II: Changing the agenda*. Birmingham: BILD

Paterson, B, Bradley, P, Stark, C, Saddler, D and Allen, D (2003) Deaths associated with restraint use in health and social care in the United Kingdom: the results of a preliminary survey. *Journal of Psychiatric and Mental Health Nursing*, 10, 3–15

R (C) v A Local Authority and Others [2011]
EWHC 1539 (Admin)

RK v BCC [2011] EWCA Civ 1305

United Nations (2006) *Convention on
the Rights of Persons with Disabilities
and Optional Protocol*. New York, NY:
United Nations

Wolfensberger, W (1972) *The Principle of
Normalization in Human Services*. Toronto:
National Institute on Mental Retardation

Wolfensberger, W (1980) The definition
of normalization: update, problems,
disagreements, and misunderstandings.
In: Flynn, R J and Nitsch, K E (eds)
*Normalization, Social Integration
and Community Services*.
Baltimore, MD: University Park Press

Wooderson, J (2010) *Reducing the Risks
Associated with the use of Physical Restraint*.
Ipswich: Centre of Excellence for Behaviour
Support

Chapter 4

Replacing restraint: good practices in North American human service programmes for persons with intellectual disabilities and autism

Bob Bowen and Simon Kemp

Introduction

The purpose of this chapter is to identify those practices that have resulted in marked reductions in the use of seclusion and restraint in services for people with intellectual disabilities and autism spectrum disorders. We have joined the diagnostic classifications of autism spectrum disorders (ASD) and intellectual disabilities (ID) for the sake of discussion, understanding a diagnosis, in our opinion, does not define who people are, but rather affects what people do. Whilst the application of good practices will vary from group to group and, indeed from person to person, the underpinning ethics, values and vision should not change as they are applied to people whose differences from each other are not nearly as great as their similarities with each other as people.

The title of the chapter comes from the concept that to reduce a specific behaviour, one must teach a replacement behaviour that is at least as effective, if not more so, in helping people to escape and/or acquire the antecedent, than the effectiveness of the behaviour to be replaced. The use of restraint can be seen as a response on the part of staff to achieve their goal of acquiring safety for themselves and/or others, and/or escaping from the threat of harm to themselves and/or others. What we have done is to ask this question: How can we support staff in acquiring safety and, at the same time, escaping from harm?

In assessing what organisations across the United States and Canada have done to reduce, if not eliminate the use of restraint, we have identified 13 specific ideas that have resulted in reducing the use of seclusion and restraint in programmes serving individuals affected by ID and ASD. A fourteenth concept, that of leadership, underpins all the others and, without it, they will have little, if any, value or impact.

Restraint and services for individuals with autism and intellectual disabilities

Prior to the 1980's, restraint was a normative response to behaviour that was out of the norm and was, in fact, seen as a treatment for persons affected by disabilities in the United States. The British approach to treatment was solidly in the framework of the 'moral treatment' espoused by Pinel and others (Poirer et al, 2012). Amariah Brigham (Brigham, 1847) was the first editor of the American Journal of Insanity (now known as the American Journal of Psychiatry), and was largely responsible for introducing a model which sought to have institutions for the 'insane' resemble educational centres rather than medical or correctional facilities. The moral treatment movement was successful until after the American Civil War, when funding obligations could no longer sustain smaller, treatment oriented settings.

Comparing the British and American approaches to restraint use in the 1880's, and in response to the American support of restraint use, Lord John Buckmill wrote that American superintendents would *"look back on their defence [of restraint] with the same wonderment . . . that has been said of domestic slavery."* (Ferleger, 2007). Sadly, Lord Buckmill was correct and restraint use became an accepted and standard practice in addressing behavioural issues in the US.

 In 1981, TASH developed the first statement opposing the use of seclusion and restraint in which they said that restraint was not a 'treatment' and that people affected by disabilities should receive services and supports in ways that did not harm them (TASH, 2001). In that same year, the Canadian Charter of Rights and Freedoms was introduced, guaranteeing fundamental freedoms and legal rights to all citizens. These rights include the right to life, liberty and security of persons and the right not to be deprived thereof except in accordance with the principles of fundamental justice. The right not to be arbitrarily detained or imprisoned and the right not to be subjected to any cruel or unusual treatment or punishment are also stated in the Charter. People with intellectual and physical disabilities are considered equal before and under the law without discrimination. However, for some people with a severe intellectual disability the right to liberty may be in conflict with the right to security of person. Some provinces, such as Ontario have looked specifically at issues of consent and substitute decision making and it has been suggested that the legislation is inadequate to safeguard the rights of some vulnerable adults.

In 1984 the American Psychiatric Association released a report in which restraint was understood as a necessary component of a behaviour treatment plan due to the aggressive behaviour of some people affected by ID (Tardiff and Mattson, 1984). These two positions, one in opposition to the use of restraint as treatment and one stating it was at times necessary continue to play out to this day in North America. The preponderance of evidence is in favour of seeing restraint and seclusion only as safety responses and not to be used as treatment or behavioural interventions (National Association of State Mental Health Program Directors, 1999, TheArcLink, 2003, CWLA 2005, Registered Nurses Association of Ontario 2012).

The authors have both worked in human services in the days when restraint use was a typical response, and understand that what was good practice in 1980 may now be a prohibited practice. Good practice guidelines have evolved and are continuing to evolve. There is general agreement that the use of restraint is an indicator of failure of the plan to prevent target behaviours from escalating to a point where there is an immediate risk of harm to self and/or others.

There have been and will continue to be opposition to legislative and ethical arguments against restraint (Lieberman, 2011). There are those who promote restraint as an ethical alternative to non-intervention (thetruthaboutpronerestraint.com, 2008, Winston et al, 2009). However, the purpose of this chapter is not to enter the debate about what restraints are or are not 'best'. Rather, in writing this chapter we are seeking to identify good practices which have resulted not only in the decrease or elimination of restraint use in North America, but also a reduction in injury for staff and individuals served. It is also the intention to highlight how those good practice examples can be replicated elsewhere.

Leadership

Leadership is important in all service settings, and at all levels of the organisation, in order for restraint reduction initiatives to be successful. The importance of leadership has been identified in many studies and reports (Huckshorn, 2004, CWLA 2005). Grafton Integrated Health Services is one example of the importance of leadership. When James Gaynor became the CEO of the organisation in 2004, he issued a challenge to minimise the use of restraint in the organisation without increasing staff injuries.

By 2009, Grafton had reduced the use of restraint by 99.7%, and staff injuries were reduced by 41.2%. The severity of staff injuries was also reduced, as demonstrated by a 94% reduction in time lost due to aggression by clients, and workers compensation costs were reduced by almost $300,000 per year (Gaynor and Sanders, 2010). The successes experienced by Grafton have been experienced to a similar extent by all of the other organisations noted in this chapter. Whilst they are all important, without leadership to provide the vision and mission, as well as the continued affirmation of staff at all levels to maintain the vision, the individual components will be much less effective at providing for the safety of all people.

It takes more than issuing a challenge for leadership to be effective. At Grafton, Kotter's eight steps to organisational change (Kotter, 1996) was used as the model for supporting the process of achieving the goal (Campbell, 2008). The culture of an organisation will either support or impede efforts to reduce if not eliminate the use of restraint. Cultures that are seen as toxic and anchored in a coercive approach to supervision and management will have that toxicity reflected in the ways in which the behaviours of individuals served are addressed. Rather than look for the 'bad apples' leaders who are attuned to the influence of the culture look for ways to keep the barrel clean and safe (Bowie 2006, Bowen et al, 2011).

For purposes of organisation, this chapter will use the public health model of primary, secondary, and tertiary intervention (Patterson et al, 2006) to frame the presentation of good practice models. In each of the three levels, specific good practices have been identified as having demonstrated success in reducing and in some cases eliminating the use of restraint and seclusion.

Components of successful restraint reduction/elimination programmes

Intervention
- Prohibited actions
- Ergonomic assessment
- Debriefing after significant events

De-escalation
- Neurosequential interventions
- Speed of motion
- Cooperation, not compliance
- Emphasis on non-verbal communication

Prevention
- Social capital
- Quality of life
- Empathy
- Trauma informed services
- Using data to inform practice
- Meeting needs

Leadership is an essential part of prevention, de-escalation, and intervention. Without leadership the individual components cannot work together as part of a larger system. It is through leadership that the culture of the organisation can change to support the good practices enumerated in this chapter.

I. Primary intervention – prevention

Meeting needs – *"People use behaviour in part to get their needs met. When we are able to help people to get their needs met, it is much less likely that they will use behaviour to get those needs met. One of the uses of behaviour is to meet our needs (Rhode Island College, 1996). When needs are not met, people will increase the frequency, intensity, and duration of their behaviour to meet those needs."* (Mandt and Bowen 2010). David Pitonyak writes that his practice is based on the idea that behavioural challenges spring from needs that are unmet (Pitonyak, 2005), and this basic concept is overlooked in the process of identifying alternatives to the need for seclusion and restraint in organisations serving people with ID

---

and autism. The definition of behaviour suggests that behaviour is what people use to escape and or/acquire stimuli. All behaviour is understood as having a communicative intent and we have forgotten to ask the simple question: What do you want? (LaVigna and Willis, 1996).

Much of the data that is generated in showing the success of specific interventions is, in the opinion of the authors, partially reflective of the fact that basic human needs have been met within the lives of the individuals served. When people's needs are met, they no longer have to use behaviour to get their needs met! The first priority is to ensure we are listening to behaviour as communication and asking ourselves how we can better help people to get what they want and/or get away from what they do not want.

Social capital: The term 'social capital' (Portes, 1998) represents the ability of people to network with others and through those relationships leverage social capital into real capital – money, real estate, advancement, etc. People with ID and autism have little if any social capital, and it requires an investment of real capital (financial supports) in order to build the social capital of people who are lacking in this critical area. Sociologists say that one measure of a person's deviance is the number of friends they have. People without social capital are often also labelled as being different from others in their society, and raising the social capital of people, increasing their circle of friends (Perske, 1988).

Another way of thinking about social capital is simply the concept of building healthy relationships. When people are in relationships with each other and value each other as human beings, social capital is built. In response to the series of articles entitled *Deadly Restraint* (Weiss et al, 1998), the Children's Health Act of 2000 was passed by Congress and signed into law in America. In the section which lays out the required content for training curricula, the first two listed are 'the needs and behaviours of the population served, [and] relationship building.' (Children's Health Act of 2000). This model follows Maslow's hierarchy of needs, demonstrating an understanding that before social capital can be built, needs must be met. As mentioned earlier, when needs are unmet, people will escalate their behaviours in order to get their needs met.

Jim Fagan, Executive Director of Regional Residential Support Services (RRSS) in Dartmouth, Nova Scotia, Canada, began focusing on the elimination of restraint and seclusion in community based services in 2002. The term they use in their organisation to measure improvements in quality of life is 'social capital'. Fagan wrote:

"The most significant change happened in 2004 when we included individuals we support in our staff training. Since then we have had several inclusive sessions and in 2010 we had the first sessions that were just for people we support. Over the last eight years the effect of having people we support offering feedback on the training in addition to our staff has been remarkable. Perhaps the most noticeable change has been the use of language that does not distinguish staff from residents.

Most recently, in 2010, for the first time a person receiving support was certified as a trainer with us. She now participates in training our new staff in orientation and with our more experienced staff in two day sessions. Her first person perspective when offering experiences from her life has made us better trainers. In the fall we will be adding a second person who receives support to our roster of trainers, which will take us another few steps along the journey.

The changes we see as a result of the efforts of all our trainers can be seen in the relationships fostered within our direct care staff, supervisory team and administrative staff, all coming full circle to the people we support on a daily basis. Through this experience there is a more clear understanding that all people have difficulties in their lives. Supporting people through those difficulties in a way that recognises who they are as people is perhaps the most important piece of what we are all learning."
(Fagan, 2012a)

Jim also says that *"Beyond our agency, an example of the impact of social capital is the enhanced relationship between the three service agencies, including people receiving support and staff, who collaborated in the conflict resolution sessions."* (Fagan, 2012b)

Quality of life: The focus on prevention, in a good practice format, should not look at how to prevent aggressive behaviour; rather, it should focus on how to create environments in which safety is present and the conditions that may lead to aggression are eliminated (Bowen et al, 2011). David Pitonyak writes that his practice is based on the understanding that 'difficult behaviours result from unmet needs.' The behaviour that is labelled difficult or challenging is a message that tells us about the person and how they perceive their quality of life (Pitonyak, 2005).

Improving quality of life, then, would appear to be a good practice as related to the reduction and eventual elimination of restraint and seclusion. The first article conceptualising the field now known as positive behaviour support said, in part, that it *"uses quality of life as both an intervention and an outcome measure and achieves reduction in targeted behaviours as a secondary by-product of quality of life for the individual"* (Horner et al, 1990).

Using quality of life as an intervention is a central focus of the Jay Nolan Center in Los Angeles, California. Jeff Strully, the CEO of the centre, says that using quality of life as an intervention and not just an outcome measure is a:

> *". . . pre-condition for good things to happen. When we utilise strategies in environments that are not positive and person centred, then we are missing out on what is or isn't important.*
>
> *Secondly, is the match. Are the right people working/supporting the right people to do the right thing and are they doing that consistently; as you know better than me, lots of problems occur when the people who support the people are the wrong people, do not pay attention to the little details. Thirdly, is the locus of control and power. When the locus of control and power is with the staff/agency/parent (sometimes) not the person then I think that is a variable that hurts.*
>
> *Outcomes achieved:*
>
> 1) *Reduction of psychotropic medication by 83%*
>
> 2) *Reduction of special incident reports by 76%*
>
> 3) *Reduction of property destruction from $156,000 in 1992 to $1,727 in 2012*
>
> 4) *Turnover rates reduced from 100% in 1992 to less than 20% in 2012*
>
> 5) *Growth, satisfaction, happiness, etc. improvement*
>
> *The problem is one of expectations. If we have low expectations then people wind up in treatment facilities, group homes, etc. rather than their own place; we also believe in the continuum – you need to earn your way to freedom – there is a wonderful article written many years ago by Dr Collen Weick and myself on the continuum and the inherent problems with this way of thinking.*

We need to remember that mental health problems, autism, etc. doesn't go away just because people have their own place, control over their lives, the right people but the intensity, duration and frequency of the problem is diminished significantly."
(Strully, 2012)

Building empathy: Not only are individuals with intellectual disabilities included in staff training, they are in positions to do staff training along with supervisory staff, for all new employees. This increase in the social capital of individuals served has resulted in a significant return on investment for Residential Resources Support Services. Truly, an ounce of prevention is worth the proverbial pound of cure.

The Arc of Delaware County in Walton, New York, has at the board level prohibited the use of physical restraint, and at the same time provided for the safety of participants through an innovative approach known as 'Vantage Point'. All people who seek to work for the organisation must, on their first day of new staff orientation, experience life as a consumer of services. Their focus on empathy – the ability to recreate another person's perspective – provides a way of helping staff understand who they are working with beyond a set of diagnostic criteria.

George Suess, Executive Director of the Arc of Delaware County, says that their commitment to not using restraint started over 35 years ago with their previous Executive Director. In order to support this, it was necessary to put into place alternatives to restraint, and one of them is building empathy for people who are served by the organisation.

"As part of the Vantage Point programme, participants are put through a series of exercises that simulate real-life disabilities. Participants are required to negotiate the physical obstacles encountered from a wheelchair; identify individuals and locations while blindfolded to replicate visual impairments; and engage in a variety of mental exercises that challenge memory and other cognitive functions. At the same time, participants interact with Delarc staff who demonstrate their hands-on approach to care and service, which blends proactive support, constant encouragement and positive reinforcement to achieve desired behaviours, without ever resorting to physical intervention or restraints. One of the people who went through the Vantage Point programme was the Commissioner of the Office for People with Developmental Disabilities in New York State, Courtney Burke. She said 'During my experience I observed both

*constant positive reinforcement and constant check-ins to see how
people were doing. I was particularly impressed by the respect
and genuine affection shown by Delarc staff to everyone.'"*
(Delarc, 2012)

Empathy is a bridge connecting two people who may otherwise interact but not
know each other (Trout, 2009). Without this bridge, we are left to use the tools
of behaviour change in mechanistic ways that are devoid of the human contact
needed for healing to take place. Empathy is much more than mere sympathy,
it allows us to recreate another person's perspective in the same way as the old
cliché 'walk a mile in their shoes' or 'see it through their eyes'. When we are able to
cross the bridge, we find new ways to 'support people, not just their behaviour'
(Bowen, 1999).

Trauma informed services: The concept of Post Traumatic Stress Disorder
(PTSD) in persons with developmental disabilities was proposed by Ruth
Ryan (Ryan, 1994), who found that all of the people she worked with who had
histories of behavioural challenges and were treated for PTSD showed signs
of improvement. Since that time the understanding that traumatic events,
especially in childhood, can result in behaviours whose origin is in the attempt
to escape from that trauma, has become part of the landscape, so to speak, of
the human service system (Huckshorn, 2004).

Literally hundreds of organisations in the US and Canada serving people
with ID and autism have trained their staff in the approach known as trauma
informed services which is a sub-clinical approach to the concept of trauma.
It is sub-clinical in that it does not teach people how to treat the effects of trauma,
but rather *"trauma informed services incorporates knowledge about trauma,
prevalence, impact, and recovery in all aspects of service delivery. [It] minimises
re-victimisation and leads to services that are hospitable and engaging to survivors"*
(Fallott, 2005).

The two words that should be focused on in the above definition of trauma
informed services are **hospitable** and **engaging**. The word 'hospitable' has
the same root as the word used to describe a place of healing – a hospital.
Hospitable places are those which, when people enter them, they feel totally
safe. This safety is not only physical, it is also psychological and emotional. One
of the most important things organisations can do is create a safe place in which
people can live, learn, work and play. Without this safety, the teaching, training,
programming, etc. that human service organisations do will be in vain.

The second word is 'engaging'. In service systems for people with ID and autism, this refers to the process known as person centred planning (O'Brien and O'Brien, 2002) or personal outcome measures (Gardner and Carren, 2005). By placing people with disabilities not just at the centre of the process but at the head of the table, they are empowered to make their own choices for their own lives. By combining hospitable places with the power of engagement, organisations can use an awareness of trauma history to inform all aspects of service delivery.

Positive behaviour support (PBS) is no longer a 'good' practice as it is now a 'standard' practice. This is not to diminish the importance of PBS in any way. What is a good practice, however, is a PBS system that is also trauma informed. In the de-escalation section of this article, the concept of neurosequential interventions is presented as a good practice, and this requires not only a trauma informed services approach as a preventative foundation, but also one which incorporates PBS.

The Polk County, Iowa, Positive Behaviour Support Network represents 16 organisations who are committed to positive behaviour support, and have added a commitment to provide trauma informed positive behaviour support. The result is that many of the organisations have markedly reduced the use of restraint in their organisations and increased the quality of life for individuals served. By incorporating PBS and trauma informed services, the Polk County Positive Behaviour Support Network has joined at least 120 other organisations in the US and Canada that have specifically asked for and received training to implement this approach.

Using data to inform practice: There is general agreement that the old adage – an ounce of prevention is worth a pound of cure – is absolutely correct. However, knowing where to put that ounce of prevention, so to speak, must be guided by data. Risk management and quality assurance protocols are often looked upon as necessary evils in human service settings. The old adage attributed to Mark Twain that 'the best predictor of future behaviour is past behaviour' continues to be of value today. Data about past behaviour can and should guide our efforts at prevention, as well as de-escalation and intervention.

The goal is to eliminate the use of restraint and seclusion in settings serving people with autism and ID. Data can identify the risks associated with the attainment of this goal, and data can identify the likelihood that a behaviour will occur, and can identify what consequences have occurred in the past.

Standard risk management process

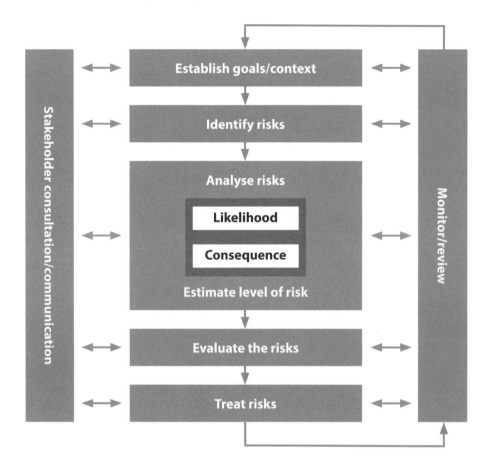

Source: Standards Australia and Standards New Zealand, AS/NZS 4360:1999

In her paper presented at a conference titled *Seclusion and Restraint – Let Risk Management Lead the Way* (Masters, 2009) poses this question: *"How come we have rocket science for distressed cardiac patients but stone-age science for agitated mental patients? That is to say, technology in other fields of medicine has moved forward dramatically, whilst little or no improvements have been seen in restraint and seclusion technology for over 2000 years; conflicting views of future of restraint lead to status quo and lack of innovation."* The data that has driven innovation in other parts of our human service system must now be focused on reducing, if not eliminating, the use of seclusion and restraint.

II Secondary intervention – de-escalation

When prevention is ineffective, de-escalation methods, it is suggested, should focus on preventing further escalation so intervention is not necessary. Lawrence Chu, a psychiatric nurse and aggression prevention trainer in Hong Kong, stresses in his work that aggression is not an event, it is a process (Chu, 2012). As such, a good practice approach to de-escalation methodologies should focus on the process and not just focus on the event itself.

Neurosequential interventions: Crotched Mountain Rehabilitation Centre is an educational and residential treatment programme for children and adults with multiple disabilities, including autism and ID. Their approach is solidly grounded in applied behaviour analysis and positive behaviour support, with an understanding that 'psychology follows neurology' (Bowen, 2011). In other words, the behaviours we use as we interact with others, our environments, and ourselves, can only follow the neurological pathways that were developed during infancy, childhood, and adolescence.

Research has demonstrated (Perry, 2002) that trauma alters the ways in which our neurological pathways develop and mature, and as a result, interventions that are centred on that awareness have a better chance of success. In writing about neurosequential interventions, Perry writes that *"A first and very important step is increasing capacity. Not enough parents, teachers, therapists, judges, or physicians know enough about child development or the basics of brain organisation and function. Simply increasing awareness of the key principles of development and brain function would, over time, lead to innovations and improved outcomes"* (Perry, 2009).

Speed of motion: When people escalate, they pay more attention to the potential threats in their environments (Ursin and Olff, 1995). Stressing to staff the importance of movements that are slow, smooth, and small is a central factor in the success of Valley Health Services in Morgantown, WV. From the period 2000 to 2011, serving over 1,000 people with ID, autism, and mental health concerns in a combination of residential, day service, and crisis response services, a total of three restraints were used.

When human beings feel more stress, their perception of threat changes and becomes more focused on the speed of motion as well as non verbal cues and tone of voice (Van den Stock et al, 2007). The quicker we as staff move, the more likely it is the person will escalate as their threat perception may interpret our behaviour as aggressive whilst in fact we are trying to de-escalate.

As individuals escalate to the point of potential aggression, staff will also escalate in their response. Under stress, our natural responses are to move quickly and with large motions. Breakaway training, for example, emphasises the need to quickly and forcefully move away from the person. However, these quick and forceful movements themselves are cue sources to the person under stress and add to their threat perception. In the process of inviting people to de-escalate, the staff at Valley Health Services have been able to consistently use slow, smooth and small movements in breakaway releases. It is this approach, added to other good practices identified in this paper that have brought about the successful de-escalation of situations and resulted in the near elimination of restraint use for over 10 years.

Emphasis on non verbal communication: When people escalate, they almost always want distance from other people. Yet when people with ID and autism escalate, many training approaches say to get closer to them in order to be in a position to respond if they escalate further. Whilst most training approaches stress stepping away from people who are threatening, most incident reports reviewed by us in our previous jobs show that staff actually step in to prevent escalation rather than step back.

Sheppard-Pratt Psychiatric Centre in the Baltimore, Maryland area, supports adolescents with intellectual disabilities. Louise Hopkins from Sheppard-Pratt, writes:

> "Let me tell you about one of our kids. This girl was so violent, there were hours of meetings about how to keep her and the milieu safe. We had changed to a different programme emphasising non-coercive approaches (line staff thought we were crazy to think less coercion was possible.) She had a trauma history that would make you cry, and she had constant, violent flashbacks. She hurt a lot of staff. When we were several months into our new training programme, one of our clinicians, who had been really pessimistic about the training, told me that this girl was getting better because she was not getting restrained. The girl would become aggressive, but then would drop to the floor. We would step away. According to the clinician, she began to realise that 'that thing' did not need to happen to her anymore, and she turned a major corner. Telling this girl we did not want to hurt her did not help. Showing her, by stepping back, was the secret."

By emphasising the non-verbal aspects of communication and inviting people to de-escalate, Sheppard-Pratt has, like many organisations, been able to significantly reduce the use of restraint. In 2011, there were no staff injuries at Sheppard-Pratt's adolescent mental health programme, and restraint use was reduced by over 95%.

Cooperation, not compliance: In 2004, the Substance Abuse and Mental Health Services Administration (Pollack, 2004) released a lengthy document focusing on moving from coercion to collaboration in mental health services. Northern Arizona University (Northern Arizona University, 2005) developed a definition for positive behaviour support which reads, in part, 'practitioners of positive behaviour support continually move away from coercion.' The paper by Kim Masters, referenced earlier, stresses the importance of an 'ecology of collaboration, not an ecology of coercion' (Masters, 2009).

Danita Achtemichuk, a teacher with the Regina Public Schools in Saskatchewan, Canada, has an innovative approach to teaching elementary school children a protocol regarding the process of escalation, and how to de-escalate. In her classroom, the children build a small 'mountain' and are able to climb this mountain physically to describe what they feel internally as they become upset. Using words and phrases familiar to these children with intellectual disabilities, the children are able to work with teachers to build a common set of words to help them express their feelings.

In this way, the teachers are able to gain cooperation with their students when the students have escalated. Using the same words as the students empowers teachers to invite students to de-escalate situations rather than comply. When people escalate, they process information through the emotional centres of the brain, not the cognitive (Perry, 2002). Any efforts at coercion will be resisted; examples include words and phrases such as 'stop' or 'calm down' or 'think before you act'. By working with children before they escalate and having them describe their own processes in their own words gives teachers the ability to invite children to de-escalate, and it is the process of inviting cooperation that de-escalation occurs.

III Tertiary intervention: Physical intervention

When prevention and de-escalation are ineffective, physical intervention may become necessary in order to ensure the safety of all people. Based on a review of organisations that have successfully reduced the use of restraint, we have identified the following components of intervention skills that have been part of an approach to reduce the use of restraint and seclusion.

Prohibited actions: One of the most important things some American states have done is to identify techniques that have high risks associated with them and prohibit the use of these techniques. The most comprehensive list we were able to find comes from the state of Washington, and contains an extensive list of prohibited actions:

"Prohibited physical interventions

1. *Physical interventions that involve any of the following elements are prohibited:*

    a. *Pain and pressure points (whether for brief or extended periods)*

    b. *Obstruction of airway and/or excessive pressure on chest, lungs, sternum, and diaphragm*

    c. *Hyperextension (pushing or pulling limbs, joints, fingers, thumbs or neck beyond normal limits in any direction) or putting the person in significant risk of hyperextension*

    d. *Joint or skin torsion (twisting/turning in opposite directions)*

    e. *Direct physical contact covering the face*

    f. *Straddling or sitting on the torso*

    g. *Excessive force (beyond resisting with like force)*

    h. *Any manoeuvre that involves punching, hitting, poking or shoving the person*

2. *The following specific physical techniques are prohibited:*

   a. *Arm or other joint locks (eg holding one or both arms behind the back and applying pressure, pulling or lifting)*

   b. *'Sleeper hold' or any manoeuvre that puts weight or pressure on any artery, or otherwise obstructs or restricts circulation*

   c. *Wrestling holds, body throws or other martial arts techniques*

   d. *Prone restraint (person lying on stomach)*

   e. *Supine restraint (person lying on back)*

   f. *Head hold where the head is used as a lever to control movement of other body parts*

   g. *Any manoeuvre that forces the person to the floor on his/her knees or hands and knees*

   h. *Any technique that keeps the person off balance (eg shoving, tripping, pushing on the backs of the knees, pulling on the person's legs or arms, swinging or spinning the person around, etc.)*

   i. *Any technique that restrains a person vertically face first against a wall or post."*

(Division of Developmental Disabilities, 2011)

It is submitted that each governmental entity responsible for the safety of individuals served should prohibit and not just restrict interventions that carry with them a high degree of risk. There are many entities that list what are known as 'restricted practices' which means that interventions that carry with them a high degree of risk can be used under certain conditions. Whilst this is an option, it does not provide safety to the staff or individuals served as the list of prohibited techniques includes prone and supine restraint, which have been demonstrated to carry high risks with them. (Equip for Equality, 2011) This chapter is not advocating for the entirety of this list; rather, a listing of those interventions which carry high risks reflects the values of the people in the community, be it a city or province or state or nation.

Debriefing after significant events: Debriefing after the use of any seclusion and/or restraint is implicitly required by CARF, an accreditation body widely used by organisations serving people with ID and autism (CARF, 2012). Debriefing is not required by federal law in America, but has been shown to be effective in settings serving people with autism and ID. In the province of Ontario, debriefing after the use of any restraint or seclusion is required, with the following standards in place:

- *"A debriefing process is conducted among all staff who were involved in the restraint or secure isolation/confinement time-out.*

- *Staff inquire with others who were in the vicinity and witnessed the restraint or secure isolation/confinement time-out (eg other persons with a developmental disability who are supported in the same area, visitors) as to their wellbeing from having witnessed the restraint.*

- *The supervisor or manager who oversees the behaviour support plan of the person with challenging behaviour who was restrained or in secure isolation/confinement time-out is made aware of the restraint or secure isolation/confinement time-out.*

- *Other staff who support the person are made aware of the restraint or secure isolation/confinement time-out (eg in the event of a shift change shortly after the restraint or secure isolation/confinement time-out has taken place).*

- *A debriefing process is conducted with the individual who was restrained or in secure isolation/confinement time-out (including individuals involved in a crisis situation), as soon as he/she is able to participate, and to the extent that he/she is willing to participate. The debriefing must be structured to accommodate the person with a developmental disability's psychological and emotional needs and cognitive capacity.*

- *Debriefings are documented.*

- *The debriefing process is conducted within a reasonable time period (ie within two business days) after the restraint or secure isolation/confinement time-out is carried out (including crisis situations). If circumstances do not permit a debriefing process to be conducted within a reasonable time period, the debriefing process should be conducted as soon as possible after the reasonable time period, and a record must be kept of the circumstances that prevented the debriefing process from being conducted within the reasonable time period.*

- *A serious occurrence report is filed with the Ministry of Community and Social Services, as may be appropriate and as per the serious occurrence reporting procedure."*

(Ministry of Community and Social Services, 2012)

Whilst this is a standard practice in Ontario, it does represent a good practice in that it is not a standard practice in most American states. It should be noted that debriefing is not an investigation. Some direct support professionals and individuals who use the service have experienced this in the past, and were asked 'why' the restraint occurred. In a debriefing process, the questions should be, in the opinion of the authors, 'who, what, when, where, and how'. These questions empower people to explain their behaviour, whilst a 'why' question creates a sense of defensiveness in people and may hamper clear and open communication.

Ergonomic assessment: The field of ergonomics is one which has, for years, been used to increase the safety of employees in many different workplaces. Occupational Health and Safety (Canada) and Occupational Health and Safety Administration (USA) regulations stipulate the need for ergonomic analyses of activities such as lifting and carrying, repetitive motion actions, etc. The authors are not aware of such requirements applied to the use of physical and/or mechanical restraint.

> "Ergonomics (or human factors) is the scientific discipline
> concerned with interactions among humans and other
> elements of a system (eg, the tools, equipment, products, tasks,
> organisation, technology, and environment). The profession
> applies theory, principles, data, methods and analysis to design
> in order to optimise human wellbeing and overall system
> performance" (ACE, 2012).

Over half of the injuries sustained by staff in human service organisations are the result of attempts to use physical and/or mechanical restraint (Mohr et al, 2003). Given that the use or attempted use of physical and mechanical restraint has such a high level of risk, an ergonomic assessment of those risks is warranted. The same philosophy and values used to require annual assessment of job functions and the skills needed to perform job functions safely (OSHA.gov, 2004) should be applied to the use of restraint.

The question about who should do such an assessment is a difficult one. Physicians may be able to do such an analysis, but their training does not empower them to assess to the same level of safety. In our opinion, the assessments should be completed by a member of the American Society of Biomechanics, which includes Canadian citizens. By requiring this level of expertise, there will be consistency in the assessment process. Design Research Engineering, an independent biomedical and bioengineering group in Michigan, conducted a thorough ergonomic assessment of The Mandt System® (Van Ee, 2004), and the US Department of Veteran Affairs have conducted an extensive ergonomic assessment of the physical skills used in restraint in Veteran Affairs hospitals (Van Male and McKenna, 2012). Both assessments were presented at public conferences and represent a commitment to safety on the part of both organisations.

Ergonomics is thought of by the general public as simply a physical science. An expanded view of ergonomics is proposed:

Expanded definition of ergonomics, figure 8-1 (Warren, 2004)

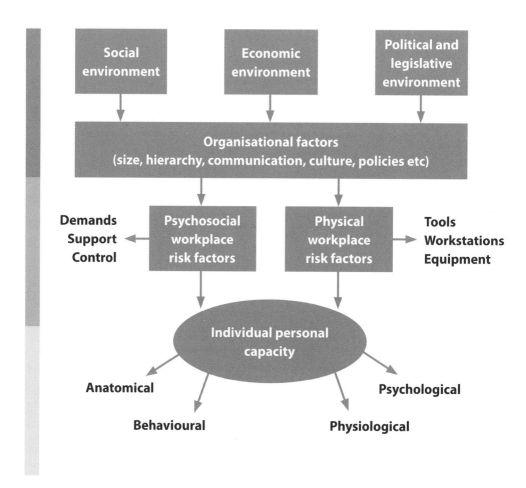

A human rights perspective on reducing restrictive practices in intellectual disability and autism

A fitting way to end this chapter on reducing, if not eliminating the use of restraint, is to recognise the importance of individual personal capacity, within the broad view of ergonomics. The social, economic, legislative and organisational factors provide the context in which the impact of good practices will move beyond a few identified examples and into the broader structure of human service systems. It is hoped that the factors identified in this chapter will provide a framework for this to occur.

The identified good practices have been implemented to one degree or another in many settings, but remain 'good practices' because they are not yet 'standard practices'. Generally speaking, the preventative components identified in the *components of successful restraint reduction/elimination* have been implemented with more consistency than the de-escalation or intervention components.

Debriefing is required in all mental health service systems in the USA, but is not required in intellectual disability service settings. The Children's Health Act of 2000 requires five of the 14 good practices identified in this chapter, but the Act was never fully enforced either at the federal or state level. Several states have implemented the five components (debriefing, trauma informed services, identifying needs and meeting them, non-verbal communication, prohibited actions), but only because the US Department of Justice entered into Settlement Decrees which resulted in the implementation of the above through regulatory action.

As reported to the authors, the most important elements that are the cornerstone of successful restraint reduction or elimination efforts are leadership, social capital and quality of life. Without these three, the other good practices would have limited, if any, effectiveness in changing outcomes at an organisational level. A common thread in all of the organisations presented as having demonstrated effective outcomes have had these three elements in their approaches. Building on this foundation, adding the other identified good practices, will result in significant reductions in the use of restraint and lead to services that truly serve people rather than coerce them into changing their behaviour.

References

ACE (2012) *What is Ergonomics and who are Ergonomists?* Association of Canadian Ergonomists. Download from http://bit.ly/1jMgD9Z [Accessed 1.7.14]

Bowen, B (1999) *Supporting People, Not Just Their Behaviors.* Presentation at the Quality Consortium Conference sponsored by The Council on Accreditation of Services and Supports for Persons with Developmental Disabilities, New Orleans, Louisiana

Bowen, B (2011) *Increased Awareness about the Effect of Traumatic Stress on Cognitive and Affective Behaviour.* Invited plenary presentation, Schizophrenia Days: Psychological Therapies in a Changing World, Stiftelsen Psykiatrisk Opplysning, Norway, November, 2011

Bowen, B, Privitera, M and Bowie, V (2011) Reducing workplace violence by creating healthy workplace environments. *Journal of Aggression, Conflict and Peace Research*, 3(4), 185–198

Bowie, V (2006) *Organisational Management and Culture as Key Triggers of Workplace Violence.* Presentation at the Reaching for the Light High Risk Interventions in Human Services Symposium, University of Stirling, Scotland

Brigham, A (1847) The moral treatment of insanity (published July, 1847). In: *The American Journal of Psychiatry*, 1994, 151(6), 11-15

Campbell, R J (2008) Change management in health care. *Health Care Manager*, 27(1), 23–39

Canadian Charter of Rights and Freedoms (1982), s2, Part I of the Constitution Act, 1982, being Schedule B to the Canada Act 1982 (UK), 1982, c11

CARF (2012) *Behavioral Health Standards Manual: Section 2F.* Tucson, AZ: CARF

Children's Health Act of 2000, Part H, section (b)(1)(B). Download from: http://1.usa.gov/1pL7ypU [Accessed 1.7.14]

Chu, L (2012) *Building Healthy Relationships: The Mandt System®.* Presented October 21, 2012 Hong Kong, China

CWLA (2005) *Best Practices in Behavior Management.* Washington DC: Child Welfare League of America

Delarc (2012) *The ARC of Delaware County Leading the Way with Vantage Point.* Retrieved from http://bit.ly/1tov2sv [Accessed 1.7.14]

Division of Developmental Disabilities (2011) *Physical Intervention Techniques.* Washington State Department of Social and Health Sciences, Division of Developmental Disabilities. Download from http://1.usa.gov/1khhcZn [Accessed 1.7.14]

Equip for Equality (2011) *National Review of Restraint Related Deaths of Children and Adults with Disabilities: The lethal consequences of restraint.* Illinois, USA: Equip for Equality

Fagan, J (2012a) Personal Communication, 1/6/2012

Fagan, J (2012b) Personal Communication, 12/5/2012

Fallot, R (2005) *A Trauma Informed Approach to Community Based Services*. Paper presented at the 7th All-Ohio Institute on Community Psychiatry, Beyond Evidence: trauma, treatment, resiliency and recovery, Cleveland, Ohio

Ferleger, D (2007) *Human Services Restraint: Reduce, replace, or relinquish?* Download from http://bit.ly/1pZ5rdR [Accessed 1.7.14]

Gardner, J F and Carran, D T (2005) Attainment of personal outcomes by people with developmental disabilities. *Mental Retardation*, 43(3), 157–174

Gaynor, J and Sanders, K (2010) *The Grafton Experience. The Minimisation of Restraint Initiative*. PowerPoint presentation, BILD International Research and Practice Conference, Dublin, Ireland, 5–7 May, 2010

Horner, R H, Dunlap, G, Koegel, R L, Carr, E G, Sailor, W, Anderson, J, Albin, R W and O'Neill, R E (1990) Toward a technology of 'non-aversive' behavioral support. *The Association for Persons with Severe Handicaps (JASH)*, 15(3), 125–132

Huckshorn, K A (2004) *Reducing the Use of Seclusion and Restraint: A national initiative for culture change and transformation*. Presentation at NASMHPD Medical Directors and NRI Inc. Best Practices Symposium, October 4-5, 2004, Atlanta, GA

Kotter, J P (1996) *Leading Change. Boston, MA:* Harvard Business School Press

LaVigna, G and Willis, T (1996) Behavioural assessment: an overview. *Positive Practices*, 1(3), 1, 10–15

Lieberman, R P (2011) Commentary: interventions based on learning principles can supplant seclusion and restraint. *The Journal of the American Academy of Psychiatry and the Law*, 39, 480–495

Mandt, D H and Bowen B (2010) *The Mandt System: Supporting people, not just their behaviors. Training manual*. Richardson, TX: The Mandt System, Inc

Masters, K (2009) Risk management. Part 1: seclusion and restraint. From: Navigating the Maze of Malpractice Risks: Let Risk Management Lead the Way, presented by Professional Risk Management Services, Inc. *Audio Digest Psychiatry*, 38(6)

McKevitt, B C and Braaksma, A D (2008) Best practices in developing a positive behavior support system at the school level. *Best Practices in School Psychology V*, 44(3), 735-748

Ministry of Community and Social Services (2012) *Policy Directives for Service Agencies, Supporting People with Challenging Behaviour*. Download from: http://bit.ly/1iZMA3u [Accessed 1.7.14]

Mohr, W K, Petti, T A and Mohr, B D (2003) Adverse effects associated with physical restraint. *Canadian Journal of Psychiatry*, 48(5) 330–337

National Association of State Mental Health Program Directors (1999) *Position Statement on Seclusion and Restraint*. Approved by the NASMHPD membership July 13, 1999

Northern Arizona University (2005). *An Overview of Positive Behavior Support.* Retrieved from Download from: http://bit.ly/1wUNhMK [Accessed 1.7.14]

O'Brien, L C and O'Brien, J (2002) The origins of person-centered planning: a community of practice perspective. In: Holburn, S and Vietze, P (eds) *Research and Practice in Person-Centered Planning.* Baltimore: Paul H Brookes Publishing Co

OSHA.gov (2004) *Training Requirements in OSHA Standards and Training Guidelines.* Download from: https://www.osha.gov/Publications/2254.html [Accessed 1.7.14]

Patterson, B, Leadbetter, D and Miller, G (2006) Preventing violence in residential care: a public health perspective. *Residential Group Care Quarterly,* 7(1), 11–13

Perry, B D (2002) *Brain Structure and Function I.* Download from: http://bit.ly/Y7LZnt [Accessed 1.7.14]

Perry, B D (2009) Examining child maltreatment through a neuro-developmental lens: clinical applications of the neurosequential model of therapeutics. *Journal of Loss and Trauma,* 14, 240–255

Perske, R (1988) *Circle of Friends.* New York: Abingdon Press

Pitonyak, D (2005) *10 Things you can do to Support a Person with Difficult Behaviors.* Download from http://www.dimagine.com [Accessed 1.7.14]

Poirer, J, Clarac, F, Barbara, J-G and Brousolle, E (2012) Figures and institutions of the neurological sciences in Paris from 1800 to 1950. Part IV: psychiatry and psychology. *Revue Neurologique,* 168, 389–402

Pollack, D A (2004) *Moving from Coercion to Collaboration in Mental Health Services.* DHHS Publication No. (SMA) 04-3869. Rockville, MD: Center for Mental Health Services, Substance Abuse and Mental Health Services Administration

Portes, J (1998) Social capital: its origins and applications in modern sociology. *Annual Review of Sociology,* 24, 1-24

Registered Nurses Association of Ontario (2012) *Promoting Safety: Alternative approaches to the use of restraints.* International Affairs and Best Practice Guidelines, Clinical Best Practice Guidelines. Toronto, ON: Registered Nurses Association of Ontario

Rhode Island College (1996). *A Functional Analysis and Positive Behavior Support Training Manual.* Providence, RI: Rhode Island College

Ryan, R (1994) Posttraumatic stress disorder in persons with developmental disabilities. *Community Mental Health Journal,* 3 (1), 45–54

Strully J (2012) Personal communication, 05/11/2012

Tardiff, K and Mattson, M R (1984) A survey of state mental health directors concerning guidelines for seclusion and restraint. In: Tardiff, K (ed) *The Psychiatric Uses of Seclusion and Restraint,* 141–150. Washington DC: American Psychiatric Press

TASH (2001) *TASH Resolution Opposing the Use of Aversive and Restrictive Procedures.* Download from: http://bit.ly/YUl2D5 [Accessed 1.7.14]

TheArcLink (2003) *Positive Behavior Supports Guidelines.* Download from: http://bit. ly/1AoUnDP [Accessed 1.7.14]

thetruthaboutpronerestraint.com (2008) www.thetruthaboutpronerestraint.com

Trout, J D (2009) *Bridging the Empathy Gap: an interview with J D Trout.* Download from http://bit.ly/1lVVwqg [Accessed 1.7.14]

Ursin, H and Olff, M (1995) Aggression, defense, and coping in humans. *Aggressive Behavior*, 21(1), 13–19

Van den Stock, J, Righart, R and de Gelde, B (2007) Body expressions influence recognition of emotions in the face and voice. *Emotion*, 7(3), 487–494

Van Ee, C (2004) *A Biomechanical Assessment and Review of the Physical Restraint Techniques of The Mandt System®.* Download from http://bit.ly/1043Qku [Accessed 1.7.14]

Van Male, L and McKenna, K (2012) *Transatlantic Collaboration in Evaluating the Science and Effectiveness of Training.* Presented at the Third International Conference on Violence in the Health Sector, October 22-24, 2012, Vancouver, BC

Warren, N (2004) The expanded definition of ergonomics. In: Sanders, M J (ed) *Ergonomics and the Management of Musculoskeletal Disorders, second edition.* St Louis, MO: Butterworth/Heinemann

Weiss E M et al (1998) *Deadly Restraint: A Hartford Courant Investigative Report.* Download from: http://bit.ly/1AfY7k3 [Accessed 1.7.14]

Winston, M, Fleisig, M and Winston, L (2009) *The Premature Call for a Ban on Prone Restraint: A detailed analysis of the issues and the evidence.* Download from: http://bit.ly/1sY4TZf [Accessed 1.7.14]

Chapter 5

Good practices in Australia in the use of restraint reduction practices for people with intellectual disabilities and autism

Lynne Webber, Jeffrey Chan and Phillip French

Background

Victoria is the second largest state in Australia with a population of 5.6 million people (Australian Bureau of Statistics, 2012). In 2006 the Victorian Parliament enacted innovative legislation, the Disability Act 2006 which established the role of the Senior Practitioner (a statutory body) responsible for protecting the rights of people with a disability, who are subject to restrictive interventions and who receive a government funded service. Importantly, as a driver for change, it required population monitoring and public reporting of the use of restrictive practices in disability services. The Disability Act also mandates research into the use of restrictive interventions, and the provision of education to personnel involved in supporting people with a disability including human rights and positive behaviour support (PBS). The inclusion of research and education as mandatory functions of the Senior Practitioner in the Act means that it is possible to focus on the evidence collected (data) by the Senior Practitioner and to directly inform policy and practice in disability services. Rarely does applied research directly inform policy and practice, because the research is often conducted by other groups (researchers) whose findings may or may not be read by policy makers and translated into practice. Making research mandatory within the legislative framework means that it is possible to examine factors that lead to the use of restraint and seclusion on a population level and to examine the impact of behaviour support planning on the use of restraint and seclusion. The research findings from Victoria are unique and are beginning to have a profound impact on policy and practice, and ultimately on the lives of people with a disability living in the state of Victoria. The purpose of this chapter is to describe the impact of this legislation and the social, political and environmental factors that are contributing to the reduction in restrictive interventions.

In this chapter we present evidence that Victoria's success in reducing the use of restraint and seclusion in disability services is not the result of a single intervention, but the consequence of a broad-based structural response to the issue made possible by the Disability Act 2006 which established the role of Senior Practitioner and provided that office and its staff with a range of functions and powers that have enabled it to intervene at both the individual and systemic levels. We present the findings on restraint and seclusion reduction over a two-year period (2008-2010) and provide evidence for the efficacy of structural interventions implemented by the Senior Practitioner and team. We also claim that at least two other peripheral structural factors: positive behaviour support and person centred active support practice frameworks and the enactment of the United Nations Convention on the Rights of Persons with Disabilities (CRPD) 2006 and Victoria's Charter of Human Rights and Responsibilities Act 2006 (United Nations, 2006) had an impact on disability support workers practice. Finally, we describe the remaining challenges and suggest initiatives that would assist in the further reduction in the use of restrictive practices in this jurisdiction.

The legislation: The Disability Act 2006

The Disability Act 2006 establishes the role of the Senior Practitioner and describes the functions of the Senior Practitioner. These functions include the monitoring and evaluation of the use of restrictive interventions and behaviour support, educating and informing service providers about how best to support people who engage in challenging behaviour, and the conduct of research into the use of restrictive interventions and compulsory treatment orders. The Disability Act also specifies that all restrictive interventions that are administered by disability services must be reported to the Senior Practitioner on a monthly basis. These restrictive interventions include any use of chemical, mechanical restraint and seclusion. Chemical restraint is defined as the use of medications where the primary purpose is to control a person's behaviour. This precludes the use of medications for treating an identified/diagnosed illness or medical condition. Mechanical restraint is defined as the use of any material (such as

A human rights perspective on reducing restrictive practices in intellectual disability and autism

gloves or socks) to control a person's movement. This precludes devices used for therapeutic purposes or to enable safe transportation (such as a buckle guard on a seatbelt in a car). Seclusion is defined as the sole confinement of a person with a disability at any hour of the day or night in any room or area where disability services are being provided. In addition, the Act specifies that any person who administers restraint and/or seclusion must have a behaviour support plan in place for the individual subject to that intervention that specifies how the restraint would be used and the ways the person will be supported appropriately. Disability service providers are required to provide a copy of the plan to the Senior Practitioner prior to using any restraint or seclusion.

The Disability Act 2006 is quite specific about the roles and functions of the Senior Practitioner and disability service providers in relation to restrictive practices. In particular, it ensures that behaviour support plans must be developed under supervision from the disability service, and that the behaviour support plans developed are subject to supervision by the Senior Practitioner. It also provides a strong basis for the collection and use of population level data and it provides the basis upon which this information may be re-invested in practice improvement. Nevertheless, Victoria's success in reducing restrictive practices is not only based on the capabilities arising from the legislation, important those these are. Ultimately, they also result from the assertive, intelligent, strategic use of these functions and powers by the Senior Practitioner and their team, including the strategic alignment of their work with broader human rights imperatives.

The Senior Practitioner and team in Victoria

The first Senior Practitioner appointed was a clinician with a high level of expertise in the area of disability services. He recruited a highly specialised group of professionals with skills in research, systems management, clinical and forensic psychology and allied health areas. The team has provided both individual and structural interventions to disability services that have been demonstrated to impact positively in a reduction in their use of restraint and seclusion. Structural approaches include the development and application of policies or programmes that are aimed at changing the conditions under which people work. They have been used successfully in public health to change the behaviour of individuals (Blankenship et al, 2006; Rao Gupta et al, 2008). While individual-focused approaches assume that the relationship between individuals and society is one in which individuals have considerable autonomy to make and act on their choices, structural approaches view individual agency as constrained by structures (Blankenship et al, 2006). According to Rao Gupta et al (2008) when a structural approach is taken, it can result in activities or services delivered to individuals, but the approach is more effective than individual interventions because it addresses factors affecting individual behaviour.

Individual interventions provided by the Senior Practitioner and their team include site visits by clinicians, advice regarding alternatives to restraint and seclusion and robust feedback to disability services using restraint and seclusion about their practice. In addition, several major structural interventions have been implemented by the Senior Practitioner to date:

(1) Data regarding the use of restraint and seclusion is collected monthly online using a standard reporting system.

(2) A standard behaviour support plan template that includes the main aspects of behaviour support planning is provided to all disability support services for their use.

(3) The development of a short online course that describes how to develop behaviour support plans for people who engage in challenging behaviours is offered to all disability support workers in Victoria by one of the professional disability bodies in Victoria.

In addition, the Senior Practitioner's team worked with the Victorian Government's disability services, Workforce Development and Learning Unit to produce a three day course on PBS that was subsequently offered to all disability support workers in the State.

The Senior Practitioner and their team have also worked with professional groups such as the Australian Psychological Society to produce a practice guide for psychologists regarding evidence-based approaches to challenging behaviours that promotes the use of psychosocial interventions as alternatives to restrictive interventions (Australian Psychological Society, 2009). They also designed and developed an online course on PBS in collaboration with Disability Professionals, Victoria. Joint work is currently underway with the Royal Australasian and New Zealand College of Psychiatrists to develop standards for psychiatrists working with people with a disability who engage in challenging behaviours.

There is a strong applied research agenda adopted by the Senior Practitioner, in which data is collected for the purposes of informing policy and practice. The data collected is analysed for patterns, trends and other factors of interest or concern, and any findings are used to inform practice and workforce development. Findings are reported back to services providers at local meetings and national conferences. Findings are also used to make structural changes to the data system to improve reporting and to build the capacity of service providers to provide quality behaviour support planning for their clients, with an emphasis on building capacity for positive behaviour support.

In addition, the Senior Practitioner sponsors large research grants (up to $50,000 AUD) and 'small change' projects (up to $2000), lead by disability support workers, to implement positive changes in their own practices related to the support of an individual who is subjected to restraint and/or seclusion. Further, the Senior Practitioner sponsors visits by leading researchers in restraint and seclusion prevention from other countries. As a direct result, two major international collaboration projects have been completed to date: (1) the use of mindfulness to reduce restraint and seclusion in disability services (Brooker et al, 2013); and (2) the use of organisational strategies to reduce restraint and seclusion (Chan et al, 2012). Currently a project is underway to pilot an organisational change strategy in disability services: 'Roadmap towards restraint and seclusion prevention'. The Roadmap uses the six core strategies demonstrated to lead to restraint and seclusion reduction in mental health services in the USA (Huckshorn, 2006) and a human rights framework to deliver an organisationally driven practice model of positive behaviour and person centred active support.

It should be noted that the establishment of the Senior Practitioner was not a totally new concept for disability service organisations. There had existed prior to this time the Intellectual Disability Review Panel that was also responsible for monitoring the use of restraint and seclusion in disability services and protecting the rights of people with a disability through reviewing decisions on the use of restrictive practices. While both the Senior Practitioner and the Intellectual Disability Review Panel collected information about the use of restraint and seclusion, the Disability Act 2006 made this reporting and monitoring more rigorous than the Act it replaced, The Intellectually Disabled Persons' Services Act 1986. The panel did not have any powers to intervene in situations of non-compliance with legislative requirements and was reliant on receipt of an application for review by the person with a disability or his/her representative to be able to review the use of restraint and seclusion and make recommendations for practices to change or cease.

In summary, the Senior Practitioner and their team use data collected from disability services and staff to develop education and information for the disability sector in Victoria. Both individual and structural strategies are used to build the capacity of disability support services and their workers to deliver quality positive behaviour support to people at risk of restrictive interventions.

As will be seen in the next section, the success of these strategies to date has been mixed.

Restraint and seclusion in Victoria 2008-2010: The main findings

In 2008 approximately 32,200 people with a cognitive impairment (intellectual disability and or acquired brain injury) were supported by the Victorian government (Victorian National Minimum dataset 2008-09 to 2010-11) and monitored by the Office of the Senior Practitioner (Office). Approximately 6% of this group were reported to be subject to one or more restrictive interventions (Webber et al, 2011a). In 2010 approximately 5% of the population of people receiving a government funded disability service were subjected to restrictive interventions (a reduction of approximately 320 individuals subject to restrictive interventions in two years). Nevertheless, results overall were mixed. The results also showed that over the two years some types of restraint and seclusion had decreased, but some types had stayed the same or increased.

During this period, the number of people subjected to routine chemical restraint (medication administered on a regular basis) increased, while the number of people administered mechanical restraint had remained the same. However, the number of people who were secluded decreased as did the number of people administered PRN (as needed) chemical restraint. In addition, the results identified individual risk factors for restraint and seclusion. Having a diagnosis of autism was found to be a risk factor for both chemical restraint and seclusion (Webber et al, 2014). While the number of people without a diagnosis of autism that were reported to be subject to restraint and seclusion decreased, the number of people with a diagnosis of autism subjected to restraint and seclusion increased.

In addition to reporting the types of restraint and seclusion on a monthly basis, service providers were mandated by the Act to send copies of behaviour support plans to the Senior Practitioner for anyone who was subjected to restraint and/or seclusion. The behaviour support plan had to state what restraint and seclusion would be used and how the person would be supported using positive behaviour support. The Senior Practitioner reviews the legislative compliance and quality of a sample of behaviour support plans and provides feedback to the service provider. If the behaviour support plan does not meet the legislative requirements the Senior Practitioner will request that additional information is provided. The service provider is also provided with information about the quality of plans, and the service provider can make changes to the quality if they wish to do so. The Senior Practitioner also has powers to investigate and can direct disability service providers to cease or change a practice, and must provide assistance in developing alternative strategies for the management of the person (s 27, Disability Act 2006). The Senior Practitioner can also specify a shorter time period for the approval of the behaviour support plan (s 142, Disability Act 2006). A person with a disability may at any time request the disability service provider to review their behaviour support plan (s 142, Disability Act, 2006).

The quality of behaviour support plans (BSP) was assessed using a standard assessment tool, the Behaviour Support Plan Quality Evaluation (BSP-QE II) (Browning Wright et al, 2003). The BSP-QE II had been developed for children in the USA and validated for use in Australia with adults who had an intellectual disability (McVilly et al, 2013a; McVilly et al, 2013b; Webber et al, 2011c). It provides an objective assessment of 12 evidence-based quality components of behaviour support planning which includes:

(1)   an objective description of the problem behaviour/s

(2)   the predictors of each behaviour

(3)   factors that are supporting the behaviour to occur

(4)   environmental changes

(5)   the functions of the behaviour

(6)   alternative behaviours that relate to the function of the behaviour

(7)   strategies for teaching the alternative behaviour/s

(8)   reinforcers

(9)   reactive strategies

(10) goals and objectives

(11) team coordination

(12) communication strategies that will be used between team members

McVilly et al (2013a,b) assessed the quality of plans for a group of people in 2008 and then again in 2010. Significant improvements were found in some quality components, such as, functional assessment of the problem behaviour and the predictors and factors affecting the behaviour, but not other components. In support of the impact of the structural interventions outlined previously, improvements in behaviour support plans were found in components that were clearly included both in the BSP template and the three day PBS course. For example, the focus of the course and the BSP template was on functional behaviour assessment and this component showed the greatest improvement. This finding suggests that these two interventions were successful in leading to improvements in BSP development.

A more recent study has revealed that the quality of the behaviour support plan is associated with decreases in restraint and seclusion use (Webber et al, 2012). Specifically, the results of this research showed that for people whose behaviour support plans reached a minimum standard of quality compared to those that did not, there were significant reductions in the number of PRN chemical restraints, mechanical restraint and seclusion during the course of the behaviour support plan compared to prior to the plan. In addition, those plans in the higher quality group that addressed the function of the behaviour of concern showed the largest reductions in restrictive interventions, suggesting that understanding the function of behaviour of concern was critical in reducing the use of restrictive interventions.

These findings are consistent with a previous preliminary study by Webber et al (2011b) in demonstrating a relationship between the quality of behaviour support plans and the use (or non-use) of restrictive interventions. They are also consistent with work by Broadhurst and Mansell (2007) who found that written intervention programmes which included positive and proactive support approaches to challenging behaviour were less likely to lead to breakdown in placements than those without a written intervention programme. In addition, they are consistent with other research showing that the inclusion in behaviour support plans of components such as targeted positive interventions that focus on the individual's learning and needs, attention to environmental factors, a team approach and timely reviews, contribute to reductions of challenging behaviour (Carr et al, 2004; Didden et al, 2006; Harvey et al, 2009, Williams and Grossett, 2011). In this respect, Carr et al (2004) found that the incorporation of functional behaviour assessment (FBA), can double the success of interventions, when compared with interventions not based on FBA. They are also consistent with work by Cook et al (2012) who found that behaviour implementation plans designed for school children in the USA that contained evidence-based components were associated with reported student improvements. The work of Webber et al (2012) adds to the above body of knowledge by demonstrating that the use of evidence-based quality support components in behaviour support plans are associated with reductions in restrictive interventions. The implications of this research are clear; improved realisation of the human rights of people who are at risk of restrictive interventions can be achieved by improving the quality of behaviour support that is provided.

The results of the two studies outlined above provide evidence for the impact of the effectiveness of structural approaches on restraint and seclusion prevention.

These results suggest that two structural interventions: the three day positive behaviour support course and the BSP template had a particular positive impact both in terms of improvements over time in the quality of behaviour support and in the reduction in the use of restraint and seclusion. In the next section we look at two peripheral factors that are also likely to have impacted on disability support practice: evidence-based practice frameworks of PBS and person centred active support and the UN Convention on the Rights of Persons with Disabilities and the Victorian Charter of Human Rights and Responsibilities as policy drivers in disability services.

Peripheral factors that impacted on restraint reduction in Victoria, Australia

Evidence-based practice: positive behaviour support and person centred active support. The Disability Act 2006 was enacted at a time when there was a substantial literature on the evidence-based practice of positive behaviour support (PBS) and person centred active support as ethical ways to support people who engaged in severe challenging behaviours. PBS is defined by Carr et al (2002) as an applied science that uses educational and systems change to enhance a person's quality of life and to minimise challenging behaviour. Carr (2007) argues the focus of PBS is not on problem behaviour, but on problem contexts that gave rise to behaviours. The aim of PBS is to provide the support needed by individuals in terms of skills and strategies to improve their quality of life. Hence, PBS interventions comprise multi-elements, with a strong emphasis on prevention (Allen, 2009; Carr et al, 2002; Frey et al, 2009; Sugai and Horner, 2009) and are widely practised in human services settings other than in disability-specific services (Sailor et al, 2009).

Positive behaviour support (PBS) attempts to understand the person's behaviour within an ecological context and focuses on developing targeted strategies that address the behaviour through the use of environmental changes and skill teaching. One of the main principles underlying PBS is the emphasis on quality of life and how a person with challenging behaviours should be ethically supported (Carr et al, 2002). According to Singer and Wang (2009), the justification of the refocus in PBS on quality of life arises from the fact that a good quality of life is not readily available to people with challenging behaviours, making it a moral imperative for PBS practitioners to deliver practice and services that will improve their quality of life. Improving quality of life involves social inclusion, choice, personal competence and autonomy for the person (Finlay et al, 2008). People with a learning disability experience further disadvantage when the ecological and social contexts restrict the exercise of choice and inclusive practices or when their underlying physical and psychological needs are not well understood (Finlay, et al, 2008; French et al, 2010; Owen and Griffiths, 2009; Tarulli and Sales, 2009). Hence for PBS to be effective it must be built on a bio-psychosocial assessment of a person's needs and intervene to address these, it needs to be person centred, and actively involve the person in day to day life (Beadle-Brown et al, 2008).

Recent work provides evidence that PBS and person centred active support are both effective in producing positive changes for people with severe challenging behaviour (Beadle-Brown et al, 2008; Crates and Spicer, 2012 and LaVigna and Willis, 2012). Crates and Spicer (2012) examined the impact of PBS on 32 people in Tasmania, Australia who were rated as high priority, who showed either harm to self and or others. After the PBS intervention, 81% of clients showed significant decreases in the severity of episodes. In addition, anecdotal evidence from the implementers suggested other quality of life changes in clients, including decreases in restrictive interventions; however, unfortunately none of these quality of life measures were formally measured.

Human rights impetus for change. Another important factor impacting on support provided to people with a disability is the work that was taking place in Victoria in relation to human rights, specifically, the implementation of the Victorian Charter of Human Rights and Responsibilities Act (2006) and the United Nations Convention on the Rights of Persons with Disabilities (CRPD) 2006 (which was ratified by Australia with effect from August 2008). Nations that have ratified the CRPD and its Optional Protocol (such as Australia and the United Kingdom) are legally bound by them and they have an obligation to adopt all appropriate legislative, administrative and other measures to give effect to the rights recognised in the CRPD. The State of Victoria is also bound to the Victorian Charter of Human Rights and Responsibilities Act (2006), which incorporates into Victorian law the human rights recognised or declared in the United Nations General Assembly International Covenant on Civil and Political Rights (1996). Both of these instruments became (and continue to be) high level strategic drivers for the Victorian Government in disability policy from 2007 on. Both promoted full and equal enjoyment of human rights by all citizens of Victoria.

The purpose of the CRPD

> "…is to promote, protect and ensure the full and equal enjoyment
> of all human rights and fundamental freedoms by all people with
> disabilities, and to promote respect for their inherent dignity.
> People with disabilities include those who have long-term
> physical, mental, intellectual or sensory impairments which in
> interaction with various barriers may hinder their full and effective
> participation in society on an equal basis with others."
> (Article 1)

The CRPD applies to all people with a disability, and it mandates the social or ecological approach to conceptualising disability as fundamental to the realisation of human rights for people with a disability. Consistent with the values of positive behaviour support, the CRPD has been widely interpreted as embodying a 'paradigm shift' away from the medical and welfare models of disability to a social model of disability. Consistent with this social perspective, the overwhelming emphasis of the CRPD is on removing barriers or changing ecological and social contexts to positively situate impairment and disability as an expected dimension of human diversity and experience (French, 2007).

It is likely that the CRPD and the Victorian Charter raised the level of critical consciousness in disability support providers about the human rights of people they provide services to. In particular in the CRPD, Article 15 *Freedom from torture or cruel, inhuman or degrading treatment or punishment*, protects the person from medical or scientific experimentation without free consent and requires states to take effective legislation, administrative, judicial or other measures to prevent people with a disability from being subjected to torture or cruel, inhumane or degrading treatment. The United Nations Special Rapporteur on Torture recently referred specifically to 'severe forms of restraint and seclusion' and other restrictive practices as potential violations of human rights, and called for the 'reframing' of violence and abuse perpetrated against people with a disability as torture or a form of ill-treatment in the hope that this will provide stronger legal protection and redress for these violations (United Nations, 2008).

Another article that may have had an important impact on disability services practices is the *Protection of the integrity of the person* (Article 17). This is an emerging development in international human rights law and imposes an obligation on parties to recognise the right of all people with a disability to respect for their physical and mental integrity. Article 17 is particularly directed towards protection from restrictive practices and compulsory treatment. This was one of the most contentious debates in the CRPD negotiations. Its final form reflects an inability to agree on more detailed provisions that would have proscribed a range of safeguards against the unwarranted use of restrictive practices and compulsory treatment. Nevertheless, there can be no doubt that the basic thrust of the Article provides a powerful mandate for PBS as a positive, human rights based alternative to restriction and compulsory treatment as methods of controlling and changing behaviour (Chan et al, 2011).

It is difficult to measure the impact of current good practice frameworks and greater observations of human rights on restraint and seclusion directly; however the findings of a recent review are informative (Dyson Consulting Group, 2012). Dyson Consulting Group were commissioned to examine the impact of the Disability Act 2006 on community service organisations in Victoria (these are private organisations that obtain government funding to provide disability services). Many community service organisations reported that the greatest improvements that had come about due to the Disability Act 2006 were changes to behaviour support plans and increased consciousness of human rights. They also commented that the online PBS course was where they felt good practice had been implemented. These results provide some evidence that both frameworks of good practice and greater exposure to human rights principles has made a difference to the work of community service organisations to some degree.

Challenges for the future

While there have been significant decreases in the number of people subjected to PRN (as needed) chemical restraint and seclusion, three main challenges remain. First, the proportion of people with autism who are subjected to restraint has increased between 2008 and 2010 and continues to increase. Second, the total number of people subjected to mechanical restraint has not changed. Third, the use of routine chemical restraint is increasing.

People with autism. Our research shows that people with autism are more at risk of being chemically restrained and secluded than people without autism (Webber et al, 2014). This finding is not particular to Victoria as similar results have been reported from other countries (McGill et al, 2009). Our findings show that increasing the quality of behaviour support plans has an impact on the use of PRN (as needed) chemical restraint and seclusion. However, our results also show that service providers still require substantial support with certain components of quality (Webber et al, 2012). Webber et al. (2012) found that of plans reviewed, the majority of those people with autism had lower quality plans and the majority of plans did not specify: what alternative behaviour was required, how reinforcement would be used, the goals and objectives of the plans and how the team would communicate to stakeholders about the outcomes of the plan. Plans that do not include this information are unlikely to have much impact on reducing behaviours of concern because, if the person with a disability doesn't have an alternative behaviour to use, it is likely they will continue to use challenging behaviours, which in turn is likely to lead to use of reactive and restrictive interventions.

The results are clear, service providers need to be assisted to develop better quality support plans and this support needs to come in the form of structural interventions where possible. To this end, the current data system is being revised to incorporate more information about each of the components that are not currently included by service providers. This includes specific questions about these components, which hover over each of the components with brief clear explanations. In addition, the short online PBS programme has been revised, and plans are in place to revise the three day PBS programme in collaboration with the Victorian government's disability services workforce development and learning unit and to systematically assess its impact on disability support workers knowledge and skills and their use of restraint and seclusion over time.

Mechanical restraint. In terms of the number of people who are subjected to mechanical restraint, there has been no change over time. Individual assessment and intervention suggestions that have been provided to service providers by the Senior Practitioner's staff have had little impact. It is likely that a structural intervention will be necessary here as well to be effective. Two successful structural interventions for reducing mechanical restraint have been used in the USA by Williams and Grossett, (2011) and Azeem et al (2011). Williams and Grossett's intervention included: (1) the establishment of organisational goals to remove mechanical restraint; (2) consultations provided on alternatives to restraint; (3) the development or revision of behaviour support plans, and (4) the requirement for monthly status reports on the individuals subjected to restraint. In addition, they reported that they felt the recruitment of several behaviourally trained behaviour analysts along with improved behaviour analysis skills of the psychologists who had no formal training, also contributed to the reductions found through better behaviour support planning. They reported a significant, 80%, reduction in mechanical restraint over 17 months. The results of this study are consistent with the work of Webber et al (2012) in showing that the development of good quality behaviour support plans are necessary to reducing restraint.

Williams and Grossett's (2011) work is consistent with work by Azeem et al (2011), in mental health in USA, who showed that a combination of the six core strategies of restraint reduction proposed by Huckshorn (2007) were important for significant restraint reduction. These findings are also consistent with work in disability services in USA by Grafton services (Sanders, 2009). Taken together the results of these studies provide evidence that at least four of the six core strategies are important for restraint reduction: leadership at the level of the organisation, restraint reduction techniques and tools, data reporting and workforce development. It is possible that the other two strategies are also important; however, no study has examined the independent contribution of each of the six strategies.

The above evidence suggests that the reduction of restrictive interventions such as mechanical restraint in Victoria will require organisational leaders of services to commit to the goal of restraint reduction. It will require the setting of specific targets to be achieved and the use of specific restraint reduction techniques such as those used by Williams and Grossett (2011) in addition to the data reporting and workforce development which are already provided by the Senior Practitioner. PRN chemical restraint, mechanical restraint, physical restraint and seclusion are all restrictive interventions that service providers have direct control over and where substantial and significant reductions could be obtained. However, disability services have little direct control over the use of routine chemical restraint and this will require a different approach.

Routine chemical restraint. In Victoria, routine chemical restraint is prescribed by medical practitioners and administered by disability providers. Approximately 97% of all people with a disability subjected to restrictive practices in Victoria are subjected to routine chemical restraint (Webber, et al, 2011a). To date, disability services in Victoria appear to have had minimal impact over the use of routine chemical restraint. One of the problems is that medical practitioners sit within the Department of Health and are regulated by the Mental Health Act 1986 and disability services sit within the Department of Human Services and are regulated by the Disability Act 2006. The term 'chemical restraint' as defined by the Disability Act, does not exist within the Mental Health Act 1986 and the current view of many medical practitioners appears to be that all medications prescribed are for treatment, not restraint. Work is needed with medical practitioners in Australia to encourage them to review and recommend psycho-social interventions before using medications. One solution that could be trialled is one used in the UK by NICE Pathways (http://pathways.nice.org.uk) that provides online support for health and social care professionals including clinical guidelines, interventions, diagnostic guidance and quality standards to guide medical professionals to make evidence-based decisions for the people they provide health care to.

Another solution to reduce restraint and seclusion that has been used successfully in the USA is to obtain cross government departmental buy-in to get separate government departments to work together to provide evidence-based care and support for people with a disability who are subjected to restrictive interventions (LeBel et al, 2012). In Massachusetts, USA, *The Interagency Restraint and Seclusion Prevention Initiative* was agreed to in a charter signed by the Office of Health and Human Services and Office of Education. The development in Victoria of an agreement like this would be a step towards the implementation of policy working seamlessly across disability, education and health.

There is good evidence from Victoria and other jurisdictions that the way forward is to find structural approaches to obtain widespread changes in behaviour and practice needed to reduce restraint and seclusion use in disability services. Examples include using the extant data system to build the capacity of disability service providers to develop high quality behaviour support plans, working with organisational leaders to establish goals and targets for preventing the use of restraint and seclusion and obtaining agreement between government departments to adopt an inter-department restraint and seclusion prevention initiative.

Conclusion

Victoria's success in reducing restraint and seclusion use in disability services was the result of a broad-based structural response. This included supportive legislation, national and state level policy regarding the human rights of people with a disability, government funding for the education of disability support workers, the establishment of research projects to examine the potential factors leading to restraint and seclusion and the prevention of restraint and seclusion. In Victoria, there continues to be a shared ownership of the problem by service providers, professional associations, policy makers and researchers and a willingness by government to fund initiatives to prevent restraint and seclusion. Leadership, inter-agency collaboration, mandatory data reporting and analysis and a targeted workforce development strategy are clearly some of the critical elements to reinforce a rights-based legislation in order to address these challenges.

However, significant challenges remain, including the increasing number of people with autism who are being restrained and secluded, increases in the proportion of people on routine chemical restraint and lack of decrease in the use of mechanical restraint. Successful changes in these areas will require both inter-departmental collaboration similar to what occurs in some states in the USA (Le Bel et al, 2012), as well as the development of shared values with organisational leaders to encourage them to adopt a shared vision and measureable goals towards restraint prevention (Porter and Kramer, 2011).

Interdepartmental collaboration will be needed to reduce the use of routine chemical restraint because this is prescribed by medical practitioners and apart from disability services challenging and questioning the decisions of medical practitioners regarding the use and side effects of chemical restraint, the medical practitioners are the only ones who can have an impact in this area. Work is currently underway by the Senior Practitioner to work with the main professional association of psychiatrists in Australia in developing modules of study for psychiatrists about the needs of people with a disability and time will tell if this strategy is useful in reducing the use of chemical restraint by psychiatrists.

For reductions in mechanical restraint, a shared value strategy may be useful. According to Porter and Kramer (2011), governments and service providers will be most effective if they think in value terms and focus on results achieved rather than costs expended. Further, Porter and Kramer argue that government regulators (like the Senior Practitioner) may achieve more by focusing on measuring performance and introducing standards and supporting innovation and improvements in services to deliver the most impact for the least cost. The development of an electronic behaviour support plan that requires service providers to respond to all quality components, taken together with our findings that quality of behaviour support plans is associated with reductions in the use of restraint and seclusion is likely to be a successful structural change towards restraint prevention.

From data from the USA there is considerable evidence that six core strategies must be in place to reduce restraint and seclusion (Azeem et al, 2011). While the strategies put in place to date by the Senior Practitioner, namely, leadership, workforce development, data collection and analysis and alternatives to restraint and seclusion, two other strategies, debriefing and the involvement of the person with a disability may also be necessary. Unfortunately no research has examined which of the six strategies are necessary and sufficient and further research is needed in this area.

References

Allen, D (2009) Positive behavioural support as a system for people with challenging behaviour. *Psychiatry*, 8(10), 408–412

Australian Bureau of Statistics (2012) *Australian Demographic Statistics*, Mar 2012. Download from http://bit.ly/1mWRgqO [Accessed 1.7.14]

Australian Psychological Society (2009) *Evidence-Based Guidelines to Reduce the Need for Restrictive Practices in the Disability Sector*. Melbourne: Australian Psychological Society

Azeem, M W, Aujla, A, Rammerth, M, Binsfeld, G and Jones R B (2011) Effectiveness of six core strategies based on trauma informed care in reducing seclusions and restraints at a child and adolescent psychiatric hospital. *Journal of Child and Adolescent Psychiatric Nursing*, 24, 11–15

Beadle-Brown, J, Hutchinson, A and Whelton, B (2008) A better life: the implementation and effect of person-centred active support in the Avenues Trust. *Tizard Learning Disability Review*, 13(4), 15–24

Blankenship, K M, Friedman, S R, Dworkin, S and Mantell, J E (2006) Structural interventions: concepts, challenges and opportunities for research. *Journal of Urban Health: Bulletin of the New York Academy of Medicine*, 83(1)

Broadhurst, S and Mansell, J (2007) Organisational and individual factors associated with breakdown of residential placements for people with intellectual disabilities. *Journal of Intellectual Disability Research*, 51(4), 293–301

Brooker, J, Julian, J, Webber, L, Chan, J, Shawyer, F and Meadows, M (2013) Evaluation of an occupational mindfulness program for staff employed in the disability sector in Australia. *Mindfulness*, 4, 122–136

Browning Wright, D, Saren, D and Mayer, G R (2003) The Behaviour Support Plan-Quality Evaluation Guide Download from http://www.pent.ca.gov [Accessed 1.7.14]

Carr, E G (2007) The expanding vision of positive behaviour support: research perspective on happiness, helpfulness and hopefulness. *Journal of Positive Behaviour Interventions*, 9, 3–14

Carr, E G, Dunlap, G, Horner, R H, Koegel, R L and Turnbull, A P (2002) Positive behaviour support: evolution of an applied science. *Journal of Positive Behaviour Support Interventions*, 4(1), 4–16

Carr, E G, Innis, J, Blakeley-Smith, A and Vasdev, S (2004) Challenging behaviour: research design and measurement issues, In: Emerson, E, Hatton, C, Thompson, T and Parmenter, T R (eds) *The International Handbook of Applied Research in Intellectual Disabilities*. Chichester: Wiley

Chan, J, French, P and Webber, L S (2011) Positive behavioural support and the UNCRPD. *International Journal of Positive Behavioural Support*, 1(1) 7–13

Chan, J, LeBel, J and Webber, L (2012) The dollars and sense of restraints and seclusion. *Journal of Law and Medicine*, 20(1), 73–81

Charter of Human Rights and Responsibilities Act 2006. Victoria, Australia

Cook, C R, Mayer, G R, Browning Wright, D, Kraemer, B, Wallace, M D, Dart, E, Collins, T and Restori, A (2012) Exploring the link among behaviour intervention plans, treatment integrity and student outcomes under natural educational conditions. *Journal of Special Education*, 46(1), 3–16

Crates, N and Spicer, M (2012) Developing behavioural training services to meet defined standards within an Australian statewide disability service system and the associated client outcomes. *Journal of Intellectual and Developmental Disability*, 37(3), 196–208

Deci, E L and Ryan, R M (2008) Facilitating optimal motivation and psychological well-being across life's domains. *Canadian Psychology*, 49, 14–23

Didden, R, Korzilius, H, van Oorsouw, W and Sturmey, P (2006) Behavioural treatment of challenging behaviours in individuals with mild mental retardation: meta-analysis of single-subject research. *American Journal on Mental Retardation*, 111(4) 290–298

Disability Act (2006) Number 23/2006. Victoria, Australia

Dyson Consulting Group (2012) *Impact of the Disability Act 2006 on Community Sector Organisations*. Report commissioned by Department of Human Services, Victoria

Finlay, W M L, Walton, C and Antaki, C (2008) Promoting choice and control in residential services for people with learning disabilities. *Disability and Society*, 23(4) 349–360

French, P (2007) *The Convention on the Rights of Persons with Disabilities: Implications for the Office of the Senior Practitioner*. Paper presented at the Senior Practitioner Dignity Seminar, Victorian Department of Human Services, 11th July, 2007, Melbourne

French, P, Chan, J and Carracher, R (2010) Realising human rights in clinical practice and service delivery to persons with cognitive impairment who engage in behaviours of concern. *Psychiatry, Psychology and Law*, 17(2), 245–272

Frey, A J, Boyce, C A and Tarullo, L B (2009) Integrating a positive behaviour approach within Head Start. In: Sailor, W, Dunlap, G, Sugai, G and Horner, R (eds) *Handbook of Positive Behaviour Support*. New York: Springer

Harvey, S T, Boer, D, Meyer, L H and Evans, I M (2009) Updating a meta-analysis of intervention research with challenging behaviour: treatment validity and standards of practice. *Journal of Intellectual and Developmental Disability*, 34(1), 67–80

Huckshorn, K A (2006) Re-designing state mental health policy to prevent the use of seclusion and restraint. *Administration and Policy in Mental Health and Mental Health Services Research*, 33, 482–491

Intellectually Disabled Persons' Services Act (1986) No 53, Victorian Government

LaVigna, G W and Willis, T J (2012) The efficacy of positive behavioural support with the most challenging behaviour: the evidence and its implications. *Journal of Intellectual and Developmental Disability*, 37(3), 185–195

LeBel, J, Nunno, M A, Mohr, W K and O'Halloran, R (2012) Restraint and seclusion use in US school settings: recommendations from allied treatment disciplines. *American Journal of Orthopsychiatry*, 82, 75–86

McGill, P, Murphy, G and Kelly-Pike, A (2009) Frequency of use and characteristics of people with intellectual disabilities subject to physical interventions. *Journal of Applied Research in Intellectual Disabilities*, 22(2), 152–158

McVilly, K, Webber, L, Paris, M and Sharp, G (2013a) Reliability and utility of the behaviour support plan quality evaluation tool (BSP-QEII) for auditing and quality development in services for adults with intellectual disability and challenging behaviour. *Journal of Intellectual Disability Research*, 57(8), 716–727

McVilly, K, Webber, L, Sharp, G and Paris, M (2013b) The content validity of the behaviour support plan quality evaluation tool (BSP-QEII) and its potential application in accommodation and day support services for adults with intellectual disability. *Journal of Intellectual Disability Research*. 57(8), 703–715

Owen, F, Griffiths, D, Tarulli, D and Murphy, J (2009) Historical and theoretical foundations of the rights of persons with intellectual disabilities: setting the scene. In: Owen, F and Griffiths, D (eds) *Challenges to the Human Rights of People with Intellectual Disabilities*. London: Jessica Kingsley Publishers

Owen, F and Griffiths, D (2009) *Challenges to the Human Rights of People with Intellectual Disabilities*. London: Jessica Kingsley Publishers

Porter, M E and Kramer, M R (2011) Creating shared value. *Harvard Business Review*, Jan-Feb, 2–17

Rao Gupta, G, Parkhurst, J O, Ogden, J A, Aggleton, P and Mahal, A (2008) HIV prevention 4: structural approaches to HIV prevention. *Lancet*, 372, 764–75

Sailor, W, Dunlap, G, Sugai, G and Horner, R (2009)(eds) *Handbook of Positive Behaviour Support*. New York: Springer

Sanders, K (2009) The effects of an action plan, staff training, management support and monitoring on restraint use and costs of work-related injuries. *Journal of Applied Research in Intellectual Disabilities*, 22(2), 216–220

Singer, G H S and Wang, M (2009) The intellectual roots of positive behaviour support and their implications for its development. In: Sailor, W, Dunlap, G, Sugai, G, and Horner, R (eds) *Handbook of Positive Behaviour Support*. New York: Springer

Sugai, G and Horner, R H (2009) Defining and describing schoolwide positive behaviour support. In: Sailor, W, Dunlap, G, Sugai, G, and Horner, R (eds) *Handbook of Positive Behaviour Support*. New York: Springer

Tarulli, D and Sales, C (2009) Self-determination and the emerging role of person-centred planning: a dialogical framework. In: Owen, F and Griffiths, D (eds) *Challenges to the Human Rights of People with Intellectual Disabilities*. London: Jessica Kingsley Publishers

Turnbull, H R, Wilcox, B L, Stowe, M, Raper, C and Hedges, L P (2008) Public policy foundations for positive behavioural interventions, strategies, and supports. *Journal of Positive Behaviour Interventions*, 2(4), 218–230

Tyrer, P, Oliver-Africano, P, Ahmed, Z, Bouras, N and Cooray, S (2008) Risperidone, haloperidol and placebo in the treatment of aggressive challenging behaviour in patients with intellectual disability: a randomised controlled trial. *The Lancet*, 371, 57–63

United Nations (1996) *International Covenant on Civil and Political Rights*. New York, NY: Uniited Nations

United Nations (2006) *Convention on the Rights of Persons with Disabilities and Optional Protocol*. New York, NY: United Nations

United Nations (2008) *Torture and Other Cruel, Inhuman or Degrading Treatment or Punishment: Note by the Secretary-General*, UN GAOR, 63rd Sess., Provisional Agenda Item 67(a), 69, UN Doc A/63/175 (July 28, 2008)

Vause, T, Regehr, K, Feldman, M, Griffiths, D and Owen, F (2009) Right to evidence-based treatment for individuals with developmental disabilities: issues of the use of therapeutic punishment. In: Owen, F and Griffiths, D (eds) *Challenges to the Human Rights of People with Intellectual Disabilities*. London: Jessica Kingsley Publishers

Victorian Government (2012) *Victorian National Minimum dataset 2008-09 to 2010-11*. Victoria, Australia

Webber, L S, Lambrick, F and Chan, J (2011a) Preventing restraint and seclusion in disability services Victoria, Australia: one or two things that could be done differently. In: Needham, I, Nijman, H, Palmstierna, T, Almvik, R and Oud, N (eds) *Proceedings of the 7th European Congress on Violence in Clinical Psychiatry*. Amsterdam: Kavanah

Webber, L, McVilly, K and Chan, J (2011d) Restrictive interventions for people with a disability exhibiting challenging behaviours: analysis of a population database. *Journal of Applied Research in Intellectual Disabilities*, 24(6), 495–507

Webber, L S, McVilly, K, Fester, T and Chan, J (2011b) Factors influencing quality of behaviour support plans and the impact of quality of plans on restrictive intervention use. *International Journal of Positive Behavioural Support*, 1(1), 24–31

Webber, L S, McVilly, K, Fester, T and Zazelis, T (2011c) Assessing behaviour support plans for Australian adults with intellectual disability using the behavior support plan quality evaluation II (BSP-QE II). *Journal of Intellectual and Developmental Disability*, 36, 1–5

Webber, L, McVilly, K, Stevenson, E and Chan, J (2010) The use of restrictive interventions in Victoria, Australia: population data for 2007-2008. *Journal of Intellectual and Developmental Disability*, 35(3), 199–206

Webber, L, Ramcharan, P and McLean, D (2010) Minimising restraint: a case study. *Intellectual Disability Australasia*, 31, 12–15

Webber, L S, Richardson, B and Lambrick, F, (2014) Individual and organizational factors associated with the use of seclusion in disability services. *Journal of Intellectual and Developmental Disability*. Published online 16 July 2014, http://bit.ly/1qNofoT

Webber, L S, Richardson, B, Lambrick, F and Fester, T (2012) The impact of the quality of behaviour support plans on the use of restraint and seclusion in disability services. *International Journal of Positive Behavioural Support*, 2(2) 3–11

Williams, D E and Grossett, D L (2011) Reduction of restraint of people with intellectual disabilities: an organisational behavior management (OBM) approach. *Research in Developmental Disabilities*, 32, 2336–2339

Chapter 6

Conclusion: good practice

Sam Karim

Reducing the use of seclusion and restrictive practices in health, social care and educational settings is important in all of the jurisdictions covered by this book. Unfortunately, it appears to be part of human nature that significant change often occurs only when matters go awfully wrong. For example in 2008 in Georgia, USA, a 13-year-old boy hanged himself in a seclusion room with a cord a teacher had given him to hold up his trousers; this lead to a Federal debate on the use of isolation rooms (CNN, 2008). In England the BBC Panorama programme on Winterbourne View (BBC, 2011), that showed evidence of the abusive use of restrictive physical intervention, lead to public outcry and a call for action by the government, care providers, regulators and others.

In relation to seclusion and isolation, case law in England is helping to set out what is acceptable and unacceptable practice in relation to the use of restrictive physical interventions. The case of *A Local Authority v. C* [2011] EWHC 1539 (Admin) ('the C case') brought to light evidence that some institutions use 'isolation rooms' to manage severe challenging behaviour. This means isolating somebody in a room and not allowing them to exit until their behaviour has 'improved'. Notwithstanding the serious conclusion that C was unlawfully deprived of his liberty (for a period that was never determined), the judgment remains of utmost importance for all those involved in caring for individuals with severe challenging behaviour. But this was not for any want of guidance produced by the government, indeed, the judge concluded that, *"…. despite the plethora of government guidance and regulation, the court is left with a worrying impression that urban myth and so called 'common sense' rather than expert advice and multi-disciplinary working practices continue to be influential in some residential settings."*

Sadly the abusive use of restrictive physical interventions, including the use of seclusion and isolation has been reported over many years in many countries.

In England and Wales, in the 1980s and 1990s, the use of restrictive physical interventions to manage challenging behaviour led to public objections and campaigning to improve policies and training in the use of physical techniques. In 1999 a BBC television programme MacIntyre Undercover (BBC, 1999) highlighted the use of restraints in care homes for people with intellectual disabilities. This led to the government working with BILD and the National Autistic Society to produce *Physical Interventions: A Policy Framework* (Harris et al, 1996) and later in 2002 the guidance for adult and children's services in England (Department of Health and Department for Education and Skills, 2002).

Similarly in the USA, leaders in the field, in *Reducing the Use of Seclusion and Restraint* (National Association of State Mental Health Program Directors, 1999) called for the reduction of restraint and seclusion and suggested six principle strategies: leadership and organisational change, the use of data to inform practice, workforce development, the use of seclusion and restraint prevention tools, consumer roles in inpatient settings and debriefing.

This book has considered a number of differing experiences and approaches throughout the various jurisdictions. In an attempt to draw the threads together, it is argued that good practice can be summarised under these strands – the legal underpinning, guidance and the operational detail. These three stands will now be explored in more detail.

Legal underpinning

Whenever health, social care or education organisations in any legal jurisdiction, are considering the possible use of a restrictive physical intervention this should always be done in full consideration of the existing legislative framework. The use of unlawful restrictive physical intervention on children and adults who lack capacity may constitute an offence of, for example, assault, false imprisonment or in more serious cases, grievous bodily harm. It is clear from the statutory frameworks discussed in earlier chapters that the issue of restraint is an important one, which should be dealt with in a comprehensive manner to protect the rights of the individual and to avoid any assertion that the organisation or its employees have acted unlawfully.

Whilst there are of course situations where the use of restrictive physical intervention is the appropriate step to take in order to act in an individual's best interests, I am certainly of the view that early intervention and positive behaviour management leads to an improved quality of life for the individual and a decreased requirement to implement restrictive measures.

The British Institute of Learning Disabilities' book *Physical Interventions and the Law* (Lyon and Pimor, 2004) and other BILD publications (Allen, 2011, Paley-Wakefield, 2013 and Jefferson, in press) clearly argue that efforts should be made to minimise the use of restraint where possible by use of primary and secondary prevention strategies. Primary prevention include a change in aspects of the individual's living and social environment to reduce the likelihood of challenging behaviour whereas secondary prevention aims to stop the behaviour from escalating once triggered.

It is suggested in the Department of Health and Department for Education and Skills (2002) guidance that primary prevention can be achieved by the following:

- ensuring that the number of staff deployed and their level of competence corresponds to the needs of the incapacitated individual and the likelihood that physical interventions will be needed

- helping the incapacitated individual to avoid situations which are known to provoke violent or aggressive behaviour

- developing care plans which are responsive to the individual needs

- creating opportunities for individuals to engage in meaningful activities which include opportunities for choice and a sense of achievement

- talking to individuals, their families and advocates about the way in which they prefer to be managed when they pose a significant risk to themselves or others, eg some individuals prefer withdrawal to a quiet area to an intervention which involves bodily contact

In relation to secondary prevention, the guidance confirms that this is achieved by recognising the early stages of a behavioural sequence that is likely to develop into violence or aggression and employing diffusion techniques to avert any further escalation.

Paragraphs 10.7 and 10.8 of the guidance sets out that any use of physical intervention must be regulated by a specific internal policy. The policy should outline what steps should be taken and exhausted before the use of physical restraint and all care practitioners should abide by such policy. The guidance specifies that the local policy should include the following:

- strategies for preventing the occurrence of behaviours which precipitate the use of a physical intervention

- strategies for de-escalation or diffusion which can avert the need for a physical intervention

- procedures for post incident support and debriefing for staff, children, individuals and their families

It is clear form the chapters in this book that national legislation and guidance on human rights and the use of restrictive practices play a significant role in reducing the use of restrictive interventions.

The guidance

In relation to the use of restrictive practices including the use of seclusion and physical intervention, this area is one which does benefit from clear national guidance in the countries covered in this publication. In England for example, there are several significant documents that set out circumstances in which restraint and seclusion are permissible, and what steps are required to be taken to ensure it is lawful. These include the *Code of Practice: Mental Health Act 1983* (Department of Health, 2008) and the recent guidance for services supporting adults, *Positive and Proactive Care: Reducing the need for restrictive interventions* (Department of Health, 2014).

Code of Practice: Mental Health Act 1983

The general use of seclusion and its meaning is defined by the revised *Code of Practice: Mental Health Act 1983* (Department of Health, 2008) ('the Code'), which defines seclusion as, *"..... the supervised confinement of a patient in a room. Its sole aim is to contain severely disturbed behaviour which is likely to cause harm to others"* (Paragraph 15.43).

The revised Code does not elaborate further on the use of seclusion. Previously, advice had been that it should:

- never take place in a locked room

- be a practice wholly distinguished from seclusion

- be one part of a range of approaches

- not take place in a seclusion room

- be clearly defined within policy

- enable the 'patient' to lead a less restricted life

- be part of a treatment plan leading towards the achievement of
  positive goals

Chapter 18 of *Mental Health Act Code of Practice* dated 1999

Chapter 15 is of particular importance in relation to seclusion. It states:

"15.43 *Seclusion is the supervised confinement of a patient in a room, which may be locked. Its sole aim is to contain severely disturbed behaviour which is likely to cause harm to others.*

15.44 Alternative terminology such as 'therapeutic isolation', 'single-person wards' and 'enforced segregation' should not be used to deprive patients of the safeguards established for the use of seclusion. All episodes which meet the definition in the previous paragraph must be treated as seclusion, regardless of the terminology used.

15.45 Seclusion should be used only as a last resort and for the shortest possible time. Seclusion should not be used as a punishment or a threat, or because of a shortage of staff. It should not form part of a treatment programme. Seclusion should never be used solely as a means of managing self harming behaviour. Where the patient poses a risk of self harm as well as harm to others, seclusion should be used only when the professionals involved are satisfied that the need to protect other people outweighs any increased risk to the patient's health or safety and that any such risk can be properly managed.

15.46 Seclusion of an informal patient should be taken as an indication of the need to consider formal detention.

15.47 Hospital policies should include clear written guidelines on the use of seclusion. Guidelines should:

- *ensure the safety and wellbeing of the patient*

- *ensure that the patient receives the care and support rendered necessary by their seclusion both during and after it has taken place*

- distinguish between seclusion and psychological behaviour therapy interventions (such as 'time out')

- specify a suitable environment that takes account of the patient's dignity and physical wellbeing

- set out the roles and responsibilities of staff

- set requirements for recording, monitoring and reviewing the use of seclusion and any follow-up action.

[...]

15.60 The room used for seclusion should:

- provide privacy from other patients, but enable the staff to observe the patient at all times

- be safe and secure and should not contain anything which could cause harm to the patient or others

- be adequately furnished, heated, lit and ventilated

- be quiet but not soundproofed and should have some means of calling for attention (operation of which should be explained to the patient)."

Paragraphs 15.48 to 15.59 of the Code set out a procedure for seclusion. In essence there is a requirement for a local policy, which sets out a procedure for starting and reviewing seclusion. A suitably qualified professional can make the decision but immediately informs others so that an initial multidisciplinary review of the need for seclusion can occur as soon as is practicable after the seclusion begins. The review is to establish whether seclusion needs to continue, the individual care needs of the person while he is in seclusion and the steps that should be taken to bring the need for seclusion to an end as quickly as possible. There are review criteria: every two hours by the suitably qualified professionals and every four hours by a doctor or suitably qualified approved clinician. If the person is secluded for eight hours consecutively or 12 hours over a period of 48 hours a more formal multidisciplinary review is to be undertaken. There are also protections about the availability of suitably skilled professionals within sight and sound of the seclusion room, the observation and monitoring of the person and a documented record every 15 minutes. Paragraph 15.62 sets out basic record keeping requirements.

Guidance on Restraint and Seclusion in Health and Personal Social Services

The Human Rights Working Group on Restraint and Seclusion in Northern Ireland produced guidance entitled *Guidance on Restraint and Seclusion in Health and Personal Social Services* in August 2005 ('2005 Guidance'). Whilst this is applicable only in Northern Ireland it has wider relevance as it has regard to the Code and the Human Rights Act. Relevant sections are included below:

"*1.12   Restraint and seclusion should be used only for controlling violent behaviour or to protect the service user or other persons. In exceptional circumstances, physical intervention may be necessary to give essential medical treatment. The decision to use either is extremely serious and restraint and seclusion should only be used as follows:*

- *as intervention of last resort*

- *where other, less restrictive, strategies have been unsuccessful, although an emergency situation may now allow time to try those other strategies*

- *never for punishment*

- *in reaching the decision, consideration should also be given to the individual needs of each service user in deciding the best method of control or restraint to be employed*

1.14   Risk assessment is an essential element in the care and treatment of all patients and clients and should underpin the guidance which service providers make available to staff. It could be argued that it is one of the most fundamental interventions in the recognition, prevention and therapeutic management of violence and aggression. The use of other interventions such as observation, psychosocial interventions or restraint should be part of a management plan based on an assessment of risk. While it is acknowledged that the occurrence of aggressive or violent incidents are not always predictable, assessment of risk, followed by a properly developed management plan is essential to the prevention and management of aggression and violence. Being able to predict who is more likely to engage in a violent act may enable staff to reduce the risk.

2.10 The issue of seclusion is particularly complex. Seclusion is an emergency procedure, only to be resorted to when there is an immediate risk of significant physical harm. There is general agreement that it should not be considered as a form of treatment; the aim should be simply that of safe containment. Seclusion is usually unpleasant, and difficult for a service user to view other than as punishment, and not a therapeutic experience. In 1996, the Royal Colleges of Psychiatry and Nursing published a joint review into strategies for managing disturbed violent patients (Strategies for the Management of Disturbed and Violent Patients in Psychiatric Units). The reason for the review stemmed from the well-founded and widespread concern about the potential for the misuse of seclusion. Concerns had focused on its use for prolonged periods of time (Department of Health and Social Security, 1980; Department of Health and Social Security, 1985) as well as on the indications for, and frequency of, its use. Matters came to a head with the occurrence of several deaths, notably those of Sean Walton at Moss Side Hospital in 1988 and of three patients at Broadmoor Hospital (Department of Health, 1993). In 1992 the Committee of Inquiry into complaints at Ashworth Hospital strongly recommended the abolition of seclusion within that hospital as well as a wider, statutory prohibition (Department of Health, 1992). Since the Ashworth Inquiry the Special Hospitals have made it their stated policy to limit the use of seclusion to exceptional circumstances and to promote alternative approaches for the management of violence. This approach is endorsed by this Working Group which recommends its adoption.

2.11 In considering seclusion there is a need to draw a distinction between:

● seclusion where a service user is forced to spend time alone against his/her will

● time out which involves restricting the service user's access to all positive reinforcements as part of a behavioural programme (this is explored in more detail in Paragraph 2.13)

● withdrawal which involves removing the person from a situation which causes anxiety or distress, to a location where he/she can be continuously observed and supported until ready to resume usual activities

2.17 The planned use of physical interventions involves the use of an agreed strategy which includes the possible use of physical intervention to intervene in a sequence of behaviours with the aim of avoiding or reducing injury/injuries.

2.19 Planned physical interventions are normally used as a last resort. Strategies designed to manage aggressive/violent behaviours should include:

> *i. ecological strategies and the environment of the service user*

> *ii. early intervention and de-escalation*

> *iii. emergency use of physical intervention*

5.5 Efforts to minimise the use of restraint or seclusion should be in place. This may require the adoption of primary and secondary preventative strategies.

5.6 Primary prevention is achieved by:

- *ensuring that the number of staff deployed and their level of competence corresponds to the needs of service users and the likelihood that physical interventions will be needed. Staff should not be placed in vulnerable positions*

- *helping service users to avoid situations which are known to provoke violent or aggressive behaviour, for example, settings where there are few options for individualised activities*

- *developing care plans, which are responsive to individual needs and include current information on risk assessment*

- *creating opportunities for service users to engage in meaningful activities which include opportunities for choice and a sense of achievement*

- *developing staff expertise in working with service users who present challenging behaviours*

- *talking to service users, their families and advocates about the way in which they prefer to be managed when they pose a significant risk to themselves or others. Some service users prefer withdrawal to a quiet area to an intervention which involves bodily contact*

5.7 Secondary prevention involves recognising the early stages of a behavioural sequence that is likely to develop into violence or aggression and employing 'defusion' techniques to avert any further escalation. Where there is clear documented evidence that particular sequences of behaviour rapidly escalate into serious violence, the use of interventions at an early stage in the sequence may, potentially, be justified if it is clear that:

- *primary prevention has not been effective*
- *the risks associated with not acting are greater than the risks of using restraint or seclusion*
- *other appropriate methods, which do not involve restraint or seclusion, have been tried without success*

5.16 There must be a written protocol, which includes:

- *a description of behaviour sequences and settings which may require the use of restraint or seclusion*
- *the results of any assessment which has determined any contra-indications for the use of physical interventions*
- *a risk assessment which balances the risk of using physical intervention against the risk of not using a physical intervention*
- *a record of the views of the service user or those with parental responsibility in the case of children, and family members in the case of adults not deemed competent to make informed choices*
- *a system of recording behaviours and the use of restrictive physical interventions using an incident book with numbered and dated pages*
- *a record of previous methods which have been tried without success*
- *a description of the specific physical intervention techniques which are sanctioned, and the dates on which they will be reviewed*
- *details of staff who are judged competent to use these methods with this person*
- *the ways in which this approach will be reviewed, the frequency of review meetings and members of the review team*

5.17 An up-to-date copy of this protocol must be included in the service user's individual care plan."

Changes in practice

What follows are some ideas to explain how health, social care and education providers can make changes to their practice so that they lawfully manage restrictive physical interventions that may include the use of physical restraints and seclusion, in exceptional circumstances.

As Paley suggests in Chapter 3 of this book, all considerations about the use of a restrictive physical intervention should adopt a positive behaviour support model of ethical decision making, which includes:

- taking account of the indicators of a behavioural assessment and behavioural risk assessment

- taking account of the environmental risk assessment

- being based on multidisciplinary decision making protocols

- including a review of the evidence base of any agreed approach

- taking account of personal, cultural and social factors that are important to the individual

- being embedded in sound organisational policy, procedural and guidance frameworks

Having regard to what has been discussed, my view is that the following are key factors that should be taken into account in reaching decisions concerning good practice:

1. The use of restrictive physical intervention including seclusion must always be based on the principal criteria of *ultimum remedium*; it is used as a last resort, after less restrictive interventions have been considered, implemented and exhausted. This appears as a central feature of the Mental Capacity Act in England and Wales when it considers the issue of a deprivation of liberty, and the guidance in England *Positive and Proactive Care: Reducing the need for restrictive interventions* (Department of Health, 2014).

2. The ethical implications of any decisions to use a restrictive physical intervention need to be considered. This includes the use of a particular physical intervention or seclusion.

3. It is recognised that isolation rooms or seclusion rooms and restrictive physical interventions are not an acceptable prescribed therapy for people with autism, learning disabilities, challenging behaviour or self-injurious behaviour. They are a means of managing behaviour and should

follow principles of positive behaviour support, namely that they do not accentuate the undesired behaviour over time.

4. An isolation room can be seclusion, ie supervised in a confined space in accordance with the definition applied to seclusion in the Mental Health Act 1983 Code of Practice at Paragraph 15:43.

5. An isolation room is a room which is not locked and which is not a confinement, and is usually used for the purpose of isolating the person from an environment that is disturbing them. The room should insulate the person from the disturbance, or over stimulation, while carers remove the stimulus. The emphasis should be on removal of the problem not placing the person in the room.

6. In some cases, the emphasis may be on removing the individual rather than the causes of his distress and irritation, eg noise in the accommodation and other sensory intolerances.

7. No room such as an isolation room, or any other restrictive physical interventions, should be used without a full behaviour support plan, which is used to instruct support staff in how to enable the person to improve their quality of life, learn new skills, stay calm and interact. This should be a holistic plan with the use of any restrictive physical intervention or a room being a small part. It should include a clear rationale for why the intervention should be used, when it needs to be used and what are the boundaries and protections to be used in each event.

8. Any person working with an individual who may need to be restrained must have attended a course on how to improve the person's quality of life, how to prevent behaviour that challenges and how, if required, to safely manage them and to physically restrain or seclude them when that is necessary.

9. An isolation room or restrictive physical interventions must never be used as a punishment.

At the time of completing the work on this publication, the Department of Health issued new guidance on reducing the use of restrictive practices, *Positive and Proactive Care: Reducing the need for restrictive interventions* (Department of Health, 2014), it covers services supporting adults in England. It is explicitly based on a human rights based approach and on the key principles of participation, accountability, non discriminatory action, empowerment and legality. Further guidance relating to reducing the use of restrictive practices when supporting children and young people in England will be issued later in 2014.

In addition to the above, it is argued that good practical approaches, as set out in legislation and guidance, should also be supplemented by the following four guiding principles.

First, leadership is often noted as a key component in reducing the use of restrictive practice. The most effective leadership involves the movement for positive change. This can be ideological in nature or the actual leadership on the ground for the reduction of restraint and isolation rooms. It could be national and local leadership. Whatever the definition one adopts, it needs to be supported by policies and procedures that set limits and thresholds for acting within the law and relevant codes of practice.

Second, is the importance of meeting the individual's actual 'needs' as described by Bowen and Kemp in Chapter 4. In England and Wales section 47(1) of the National Health Service and Community Care Act 1990 defines the process in which one can identify a person's presenting needs. Once identified, and considered to be eligible, the local authority is mandated to meet those needs. To that extent, robust primary legislation is required to ensure that services are provided commensurate to actual need. Avenues of redress are also required. To a certain degree the ability to achieve redress in such circumstances accords to the theory of social capital as discussed by Bowen and Kemp. A proper legal system, which protects the vulnerable and empowers individuals with rights, is, therefore, necessary.

Third, having said the above, primary legislation could go a step further and mandate certain minimum requirements, and prohibit certain acts or omission. In this regard, the Disability Act 2006 of Victoria, Australia, is in my view, the most innovative piece of legislation. This also connects to the human rights agenda, be it via the Human Rights Act 1998 in England and Wales incorporating the ECHR, or the Victorian Charter of Human Rights. These legislative frameworks provide an ideal basis to ensuring that basic standards are met, such as preventing unlawful loss of an individual's liberty, or degrading and inhumane treatment. The growing jurisprudence, at least in England and Wales, of ensuring that individuals are lawfully detained, when so required, is enshrined in the Mental Capacity Act, and the use of the Standard Authorisation. That, however, is only applicable to those who lack mental capacity to make relevant decisions. Those with sufficient mental capacity can challenge the lawfulness of a decision of a public body by way of judicial review. Both are routes by which a person can challenge certain practices to see whether they are lawful or unjustified, as happened in the case of C.

Fourth, and finally, as the contributors have suggested, service providers require assistance in the development of quality behaviour support plans, which could come via the use of government direction. In Victoria, unlike any other jurisdiction, the Disability Act 2006 prescribes, where relevant that the use of any restrictive interventions must be reported to a Senior Practitioner on a *monthly* basis, and that behaviour support plans are subject to supervision (see Chapter 2). The Senior Practitioner also has the power to investigate or to order that certain practices are ceased. A person with a disability can ask for a review of this plan at any time. In addition, the team provides feedback on the use of restraints and seclusion. Remarkably, data regarding the use of restraint and seclusion is collated on a monthly basis, and a pro forma behaviour support plan is provided to all disability support services, which has been developed in conjunction with the Australian Psychological Society for the use of psychosocial interventions to limit physical interventions.

In addition to national guidance, individual organisations need to provide guidance to their employees in relation to the legal and ethical use of restrictive physical intervention. Organisations do this through the use of policies and procedures. A policy should aid staff to make sound judgments and take appropriate actions that are legal, consistent with the aims and values of the organisation, and in the best interest of the people it provides services to. Procedures should provide detailed guidelines for practice in what staff need to do or know in order to comply with a particular policy (Jefferson, in press).

I sincerely hope that these final principles provide a useful source of reference, and a guide for those concerned about the growing restraint reduction strategies throughout the world.

References

A Local Authority v C [2011] EWHC 1539 (Admin)

Allen, D (2011) *Reducing the Use of Restrictive Practices with People who have Intellectual Disabilities: A practical approach.* Birmingham: BILD

BBC (1999) *MacIntye Undercover.* Broadcast November 1999

BBC (2011) *Undercover Care: The abuse exposed.* BBC Panorama first shown on 31 May 2011

CNN (2008) *Children forced into cell-like school seclusion rooms.* Download from: www.cnn.com/2008/US/12/17/seclusion. rooms/ [Accessed 1.7.14]

Council of Europe (2002) *European Convention on Human Rights Protocol 13.* Strasbourg: The Council of Europe

Department for Constitutional Affairs (2005) *Mental Capacity Act 2005.* Download from www.legislation.gov.uk

Department of Health (1992) *Report of the Committee of Inquiry into Complaints about Ashworth Hospital.* London: HMSO

Department of Health (1993) *Report of the Committee of Inquiry into the Death in Broadmoor Hospital of Orville Blackwood and a Review of the Deaths of Two Other Afro-Caribbean Patients: Big, black and dangerous.* London: HMSO

Department of Health (2008) *Code of Practice: Mental Health Act 1983.* London: TSO

Department of Health (2014) *Positive and Proactive Care: Reducing the need for restrictive interventions.* London: DH

Department of Health and Department for Education and Skills (2002) *Guidance for Restrictive Physical Interventions: How to provide safe services for people with learning disabilities and autistic spectrum disorder.* London: DH

Department of Health and Social Security (1980) *Report of the Review of Rampton Hospital.* London: HMSO

Department of Health and Social Security (1985) *Report to the Secretary of State for Social Services Concerning the Death of Mr Michael Martin at Broadmoor Hospital on 6th July 1984.* London: HMSO

Disability Act 2006. Victoria, Australia

Harris, J, Allen, D, Cornick, M, Jefferson, A and Mills, R (1996) *Physical Interventions: A policy framework.* Birmingham: BILD

Human Rights Act 1998. Available to download at www.legislation.gov.uk

Human Rights Working Group on Restraint and Seclusion (2005) *Guidance on Restraint and Seclusion in Health and Personal Social Services.* Belfast: DHSSPNI

Jefferson, A (in press) *Positive Behaviour Support: A policy framework.* Birmingham: BILD

Lyon, M and Pimor, A (2004) *Physical Interventions and the Law.* Birmingham: BILD

Mental Health Act 1983. Available to
download at www.legislation.gov.uk

National Association of State Mental
Health Program Directors (1999)
*Reducing the Use of Seclusion and Restraint:
Findings, strategies and recommendations*.
Download from: http://bit.ly/1meXBOh
[Accessed 1.7.14]

*National Health Service and Community
Care Act 1990*. Available to download at
www.legislation.gov.uk

Paley-Wakefield, S (2013) *Framework
for Reducing Restrictive Practices*.
Birmingham: BILD

Romijn A and Freveriks J M (2012)
Restriction on restraints in the care
for people with intellectual disabilities
in the Netherlands: lessons learned
from Australia, UK, and United States.
*Journal of Policy and Practice in
Intellectual Disabilities*, 9(2), 127–133

Royal College of Psychiatrists and the Royal
College of Nursing (1996) *Strategies for
the Management of Disturbed and Violent
Patients in Psychiatric Units*. London: Royal
College of Psychiatrists and the Royal
College of Nursing

United Nations General Assembly (2013)
*Report of the Special Rapporteur on Torture
and other Cruel, Inhuman or Degrading
Treatment or Punishment, Juan E Mendez*.
New York: United Nations